Regional Growth and Decline in the United States

Second Edition

Bernard L. Weinstein,
Harold T. Gross,
and John Rees

PRAEGER SPECIAL STUDIES • PRAEGER SCIENTIFIC

New York • Philadelphia • Eastbourne, UK
Toronto • Hong Kong • Tokyo • Sydney

Library of Congress Cataloging in Publication Data

Weinstein, Bernard L.
  Regional growth and decline in the United States.

  1. United States—Economic conditions—1945-   —
Regional disparities. 2. Migration, Internal—
United States. 3. Sunbelt States—Economic conditions.
4. Northeastern States—Economic conditions. I. Gross,
Harold T. II. Rees, John, 1948-   . III. Title.
HC106.5.W425 1985   330.973′092   85-6319
ISBN 0-03-062044-9 (alk. paper)

Published in 1985 by Praeger Publishers
CBS Educational and Professional Publishing, a Division of CBS Inc.
521 Fifth Avenue, New York, NY 10175 USA

© 1978 and 1985 by Praeger Publishers

56789 052 987654321

Printed in the United States of America on acid-free paper

INTERNATIONAL OFFICES

Orders from outside the United States should be sent to the appropriate address listed below. Orders from areas not listed below should be placed through CBS International Publishing, 383 Madison Ave., New York, NY 10175 USA

Australia, New Zealand
Holt Saunders, Pty, Ltd., 9 Waltham St., Artarmon, N.S.W. 2064, Sydney, Australia

Canada
Holt, Rinehart & Winston of Canada, 55 Horner Ave., Toronto, Ontario, Canada M8Z 4X6

Europe, the Middle East, & Africa
Holt Saunders, Ltd., 1 St. Anne's Road, Eastbourne, East Sussex, England BN21 3UN

Japan
Holt Saunders, Ltd., Ichibancho Central Building, 22-1 Ichibancho, 3rd Floor, Chiyodaku, Tokyo, Japan

Hong Kong, Southeast Asia
Holt Saunders Asia, Ltd., 10 Fl, Intercontinental Plaza, 94 Granville Road, Tsim Sha Tsui East, Kowloon, Hong Kong

Manuscript submissions should be sent to the Editorial Director, Praeger Publishers, 521 Fifth Avenue, New York, NY 10175 USA

Preface

This book deals with the nature, causes, and consequences of the differential economic performance of the various regions of the United States over the past several decades. Although much has been written in the popular press and professional journals about the Sunbelt, migration, economic growth, industrial location, structural adjustment, technological change, and the impact of federal spending, few attempts have been made to integrate these developments into a comprehensive overview of postwar regional change in the United States.

At this writing, the U.S. polity is embroiled in a vigorous debate over the need for a national industrial policy. Plant closings, industrial relocations, the decline of organized labor, and massive trade deficits have contributed to the concern. We hope this book will help to illuminate some of the fundamental issues at stake in the public debate over industrial policy.

Some of the material in Chapter 6 appeared originally in the July-August 1982 issue of *Society* and is reproduced with permission.

The research assistance of John Allen and the typing assistance of Jeanette Lane are gratefully acknowledged.

Contents

LIST OF TABLES AND FIGURES

TABLES

FIGURES

1

Postwar Regional Change
in the United States:
An Overview

SOME DEFINITIONS

The Bureau of the Census, for statistical purposes, has divided the country into four primary regions: Northeast, North Central, South, and West (see Figure 1.1). Each of these regions contains several geographical subdivisions. For instance, the South is broken into three constituent state groupings: South Atlantic, East South Central, and West South Central. Most of the discussion and statistical analyses in this book will conform to these census definitions.

The Sunbelt, of course, is not a census region and has no official definition. For the purpose of this text, the Sunbelt will consist of the South plus New Mexico, Arizona, and Southern California. Occasionally, references will be made to the "Snowbelt," the "manufacturing belt," or "the industrial North." As a rule such references will encompass the New England and Middle Atlantic divisions of the Northeast region along with the East North Central division of the North Central region.

Regional growth and decline will be discussed in the context of changes in population, migration patterns, employment, income, and other measures of economic performance. The reader should bear in mind, however, that most references to regional growth and decline will be couched in a relative framework. For example, while per capita income in the Middle Atlantic division is higher than that in the West South Central division, it is rising more slowly. Over time, regional per capita income as a percentage of the U.S. average has been dropping in the Middle Atlantic states while rising in the West South Central states.[1] In this sense, the Middle Atlantic can be defined as a declining region while the West South Central area can be classified as a growing region.

FIGURE 1.1
Regions and Geographic Divisions of the United States

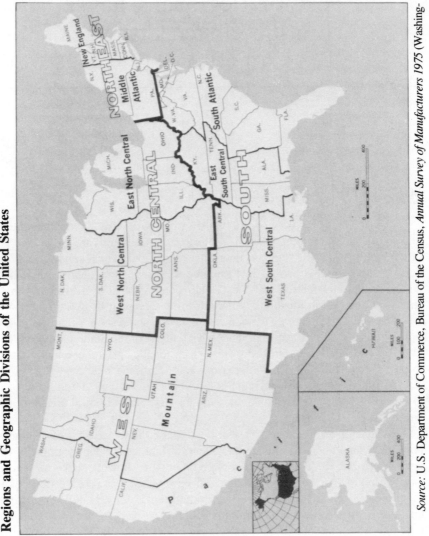

Source: U.S. Department of Commerce, Bureau of the Census, *Annual Survey of Manufacturers 1975* (Washington, D.C.: U.S. Government Printing Office, 1977), xiii.

CHANGES IN POPULATION AND DISTRIBUTION

Since 1950, the U.S. population has grown by almost 50 percent (see Table 1.1). But population growth has been decreasing steadily throughout this period. In the decade 1950–60, population grew on the average of 1.8 percent annually. Between 1960 and 1970, the annual rate of increase averaged 1.3 percent, and from 1970 to 1980 the growth rate slowed futher still to 1.1 percent.

Among regions, the West has clearly been the fastest growing since 1950, having more than doubled its population. The South has been the second fastest-growing region while both the North Central and Northeast regions have grown at rates well below the national average.

Figure 1.2 breaks down regional population growth for five periods from 1955 to 1980. In absolute numbers, the South has gained more people than any other region since 1955. Total population in the South increased by almost 27 million, compared to 22 million in the West, 13 million in the North Central region, and 8.6 million in the Northeast. From 1975 to 1980, the South grew by 7.5 million persons. Seventy-five million Americans, approximately one out of three, lived in the South by 1975.

Population growth is not evenly spread throughout each region. For instance, while the Northeast as a whole has actually lost population since 1975, certain states within the region—New Hampshire, Maine, and Vermont—have grown at rates at or above the national average (see Table 1.2). In the fast-growing South, population gains in Delaware and Maryland are lagging behind the national growth rate. Within the West region, the fastest-growing states since 1975 have been in the Mountain division.

Between 1975 and 1980 two states showed absolute losses in population—Massachusetts and New York. As a result of the substantial population declines

TABLE 1.1
U.S. Population by Region, 1950–80
(In Thousands)

	1980	1970	1960	1950	Percent Change 1950–80
Northeast	49,137	49,061	44,678	39,478	24.5
North Central	58,854	56,593	51,619	44,461	32.4
South	75,349	62,812	54,973	47,197	59.6
West	43,165	34,838	28,053	20,190[a]	114.0
U.S. Total	226,505	203,304	179,323	151,326	+49.7%

[a]Excluding Alaska and Hawaii

Sources: U.S. Department of Commerce, Bureau of the Census, *Census of Population and Housing*, 1950, 1960, 1970, and 1980.

FIGURE 1.2
Population Change for Five-Year Periods by Region, 1955–80
(Periods Beginning July 1; Change Expressed in Millions)

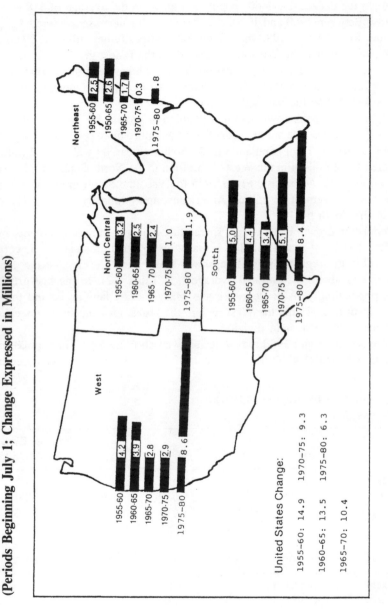

United States Change:

1955-60: 14.9 1970-75: 9.3

1960-65: 13.5 1975-80: 6.3

1965-70: 10.4

Source: U.S. Department of Commerce, Bureau of the Census, *Current Population Reports*, various issues.

TABLE 1.2
U.S. Population Growth and Components of Change by State and Region, 1970–80

State	1980	1975	1970	Percent Change 1970–75	Percent Change 1975–80	Components of Population Change: 1970–80 (in thousands)		
						Births	Deaths	Net Total Migration
Northeast								
New England	12,348,493	12,188,000	11,847,245	2.9	1.3	1,607	1,135	29
Maine	1,124,660	1,059,000	993,722	6.6	6.2	161	107	79
New Hampshire	920,610	818,000	737,681	10.8	12.5	122	75	136
Vermont	511,456	471,999	444,732	6.1	8.4	72	44	38
Massachusetts	5,737,037	5,818,000	5,689,170	2.3	-1.4	737	553	-136
Rhode Island	947,154	927,000	949,723	-2.4	2.2	123	93	-33
Connecticut	3,107,576	3,095,000	3,032,217	2.1	0.4	391	263	-52
Middle Atlantic	36,788,174	37,267,000	37,213,269	0.1	-1.3	5,055	3,534	-1,946
New York	17,557,280	18,122,000	18,241,398	-0.7	-3.1	2,481	1,622	-1,543
New Jersey	7,364,158	7,316,000	7,171,112	2.0	0.7	981	674	-114
Pennsylvania	11,866,728	11,829,000	11,880,766	-0.4	0.3	1,593	1,238	-289
North central								
East North Central	41,669,738	40,978,000	40,265,477	1.8	1.7	6,454	3,723	-1,324
Ohio	10,797,419	10,759,000	10,657,423	1.0	0.4	1,676	992	-544
Indiana	5,490,179	5,311,000	5,195,610	2.2	3.4	865	483	-87
Illinois	11,418,461	11,145,000	11,112,797	0.3	2.5	1,790	1,072	-410
Michigan	9,258,344	9,157,000	8,881,826	3.1	1.1	1,441	767	-297
Wisconsin	4,705,335	4,606,000	4,417,821	4.3	2.2	682	408	14

TABLE 1.2 (continued)

State	1980	1975	1970	Percent Change 1970–75	Percent Change 1975–80	Components of Population Change: 1970–80 (in thousands)		
						Births	Deaths	Net Total Migration
West North Central	17,184,066	16,687,000	16,327,547	2.2	3.0	2,579	1,617	−105
Minnesota	4,077,148	3,925,000	3,806,103	3.1	3.9	595	334	11
Iowa	2,913,387	2,870,000	2,825,368	1.6	1.5	432	286	−58
Missouri	4,917,444	4,763,000	4,677,623	1.8	3.2	728	505	16
North Dakota	652,695	637,000	617,792	3.1	2.5	107	56	−17
South Dakota	690,178	683,000	666,257	2.5	1.1	117	66	−26
Nebraska	1,570,006	1,542,000	1,485,333	3.8	1.8	246	149	−12
Kansas	2,363,208	2,267,000	2,249,071	0.8	4.2	354	221	−19
South								
South Atlantic	36,943,139	33,703,000	30,678,948	9.9	9.6	5,149	3,088	4,204
Delaware	595,225	579,000	548,104	5.6	2.9	88	49	8
Maryland	4,216,446	4,098,000	3,923,897	4.4	2.9	568	331	55
Virginia	5,346,279	4,966,000	4,651,448	6.8	7.7	748	406	353
West Virginia	1,949,644	1,803,000	1,744,237	3.4	8.1	290	198	113
North Carolina	5,874,429	5,451,000	5,084,411	7.2	7.8	863	468	395
South Carolina	3,119,208	2,818,000	2,590,835	8.8	10.7	498	241	272
Georgia	5,464,265	4,926,000	4,587,930	7.4	10.9	862	429	443
Florida	9,739,992	8,346,000	6,791,418	22.9	16.7	1,121	889	2,716
District of Columbia	637,651	716,000	756,668	−5.4	−10.9	109	77	−151
East South Central	14,662,882	13,544,000	12,808,077	5.7	8.3	2,301	1,309	863

Kentucky	3,661,433	3,396,000	3,220,711	5.4	7.8	568	336	209
Tennessee	4,590,750	4,188,000	3,926,018	6.7	9.6	664	393	394
Alabama	3,890,061	3,614,000	3,444,354	4.9	7.6	615	346	176
Mississippi	2,520,638	2,346,000	2,216,994	5.8	7.4	454	235	85
West South Central	23,743,134	20,855,000	19,326,057	7.9	13.8	3,772	1,848	2,493
Arkansas	2,285,513	2,116,000	1,923,322	10.0	8.0	349	218	232
Louisiana	4,203,972	3,791,000	3,644,637	4.0	10.9	717	346	188
Oklahoma	3,025,266	2,712,000	2,559,463	6.0	11.6	445	274	295
Texas	14,228,383	12,236,000	11,198,635	9.3	16.3	2,261	1,010	1,779
West								
Mountain	11,368,330	9,646,000	8,289,901	16.4	17.9	1,837	722	1,963
Montana	786,690	748,000	694,409	7.7	5.2	126	67	33
Idaho	943,935	821,000	713,015	15.1	15.0	166	65	130
Wyoming	470,816	374,000	332,416	12.5	25.9	73	31	96
Colorado	2,888,834	2,534,000	2,209,596	14.7	14.0	415	182	446
New Mexico	1,299,968	1,147,000	1,017,055	12.8	13.3	224	82	141
Arizona	2,717,866	2,224,000	1,775,399	25.3	22.2	405	174	712
Utah	1,461,037	1,206,000	1,059,273	13.9	21.1	329	76	149
Nevada	799,184	592,000	488,738	21.1	35.0	99	46	257
Pacific	31,796,869	28,185,000	26,548,342	6.2	12.8	4,493	2,305	3,060
Washington	4,130,163	3,547,000	3,413,244	3.9	16.4	548	305	474
Oregon	2,632,663	2,288,000	2,081,553	9.9	15.1	351	207	396
California	23,668,562	21,133,000	19,971,069	5.8	12.0	3,354	1,734	2,078
Alaska	400,481	352,000	302,583	16.3	13.8	78	15	36
Hawaii	965,000	865,000	769,913	12.4	11.6	163	44	76

TABLE 1.2 (continued)

State	1980	1975	1970	Percent Change 1970–75	Percent Change 1975–80	Components of Population Change: 1970–80 (in thousands)		
						Births	Deaths	Net Total Migration
Regions								
U.S. Total	226,504,825	213,051,000	203,304,863	4.8	6.3	33,247	19,281	9,237
Northeast	49,136,667	49,454,000	49,060,514	0.8	−0.6	6,662	4,669	−1,917
North Central	58,853,804	57,665,000	56,593,024	1.9	2.1	9,033	5,340	−1,429
South	75,349,155	68,101,000	62,813,082	8.4	10.6	11,222	6,245	7,560
West	43,165,199	37,831,000	34,838,243	8.6	14.1	6,330	3,027	5,023

Sources: 1980 pop.: U.S. Department of Commerce, Bureau of the Census, Supplementary Rept. 1980 Census of Population (PC80-S1-1), *Age, Sex, Race, and Spanish Origin of the Population by Regions, Divisions, and States:* 1980; 1975 pop.: U.S. Department of Commerce, Bureau of the Census, Population Estimates and Projections, *Estimates of the Population of Counties and Metropolitan Areas July 1, 1974 and 1975, Ser. P-25, No. 709, Sept. 1977 (rounded to nearest thousand).*

in these states, the Northeast region as a whole posted a slight loss in population during the 1975–80 period.

INTERREGIONAL MIGRATION

With declining birthrates throughout the nation, the most important factor in population redistribution has become interregional migration. That is, net migration—the difference between out-migration and in-migration—has accounted for a larger share of the population gain in the growing regions of the South and West (see Table 1.3). For example, in the 1970–75 period net migration was responsible for almost 35 percent of the population change in the South, although during the 1975–80 period, the figure fell to 24 percent. A similar pattern can be seen in the West, where migration accounted for 23 percent of that region's population gain during the period 1970–75 and then fell slightly to 17 percent between 1975 and 1980.

By contrast to the South and West, net out-migration has been primarily responsible for the slow population growth of the Northeast and North Central regions. As early as 1955, the North Central region was experiencing net out-

TABLE 1.3
Interregional Migration, 1965–70, 1970–75, and 1975–80
(In Thousands)

	Northeast	North Central	South	West
1965–70:				
In-migrants	1,273	2,024	3,142	2,309
Out-migrants	1,988	2,661	2,486	1,613
Net migration	−715	−637	+656	+696
1970–75:				
In-migrants	1,057	1,731	4,082	2,347
Out-migrants	2,399	2,926	2,253	1,639
Net migration	−1,342	−1,195	+1,829	+708
1975–80:				
In-migrants	1,106	1,993	4,204	2,838
Out-migrants	2,592	3,166	2,440	1,945
Net migration	−1,486	−1,173	+1,764	+893

Source: U.S. Department of Commerce, Bureau of the Census, *Current Population Reports*, Ser. P-20, No. 368, December 1981, p. 1.

migration, a process that has continued ever since. Between 1965 and 1970 the Northeast became an out-migration region for the first time.

Since 1970, the Middle Atlantic and East North Central divisions have shown the most pronounced out-migration rates, having lost 5.2 percent and 3.3 percent of their 1970 populations. Fifteen states have experienced net out-migration, and all are in the North. On balance, New York lost 1,543,000 persons between 1970 and 1980 while Ohio lost 544,000 and Illinois 410,000 (see Table 1.2).

Perhaps the most significant change in postwar migration patterns is the pronounced increase in southern in-migration beginning around 1970. In less than one generation, the South has gone from a heavy net migration loss (1950–55) to a very large gain (1970–75). By the end of the decade, the South had received over 4 million migrants from the other three census regions (see Table 1.4). The southern states had net in-migration of 7.5 million persons between 1970 and 1980 and are now attracting one and a half times as many migrants as the West.

The migration gains in the South are largely the result of net out-migration from the Northeast and North Central regions. Between 1970 and 1975, nearly a million more persons left the Northeast for the South than moved the opposite direction, and net migration between the North Central region and the South was nearly 800,000. As of 1980, Florida had the highest rate of net in-migration among the southern states, followed by Texas, Georgia, North Carolina, Tennessee, and Virginia (see Table 1.2).

EMPLOYMENT GROWTH

With slow population growth and net out-migration occurring in the Northeast and North Central regions, it is not surprising that employment gains there in recent years have lagged behind those in the rest of the nation (see Table 1.5).

TABLE 1.4
Region of Residence in 1975 and Region of Residence in 1980
for Interregional Migrants
(In Thousands, 5 Years and Over)

	Residence in 1975			
Residence in 1980	Northeast	North Central	South	West
Northeast	—	268	589	249
North Central	412	—	950	631
South	1,452	1,688	—	1,064
West	727	1,210	901	—

Source: U.S. Department of Commerce, Bureau of the Census, *Current Population Reports*, Ser. P-20, No. 368, December 1981, pp. 9–10.

TABLE 1.5
Nonagricultural Employment by Region and State, Selected Years, 1960–81
(In Thousands)

	1960	1970	1980	Dec. 1981[a]	Percent Change 1960–70	Percent Change 1970–80
Northeast						
New England	3,697.7	4,549.9	5,474.5	5,533.4	23.0	20.3
Maine	277.5	332.2	419.2	411.9	19.7	26.2
New Hampshire	200.7	259.9	384.9	390.3	29.5	48.1
Vermont	107.9	147.9	199.7	203.4	37.1	35.0
Massachusetts	1,904.7	2,268.3	2,647.8	2,690.5	19.1	16.7
Rhode Island	291.7	344.1	398.5	402.3	18.0	15.8
Connecticut	915.4	1,197.5	1,424.4	1,435.0	30.8	18.9
Middle Atlantic	11,914.4	14,116.6	15,011.6	15,041.2	18.5	6.3
New York	6,181.9	7,156.4	7,204.7	7,295.4	15.8	0.7
New Jersey	2,017.1	2,608.6	3,053.9	3,096.3	29.3	17.1
Pennsylvania	3,715.4	4,351.6	4,753.0	4,649.5	17.1	9.2
North Central						
East North Central	11,659.2	14,610.5	16,826.8	16,580.6	25.3	15.2
Ohio	3,147.3	3,880.6	4,398.8	4,341.9	23.3	13.4
Indiana	1,431.4	1,849.0	2,137.1	2,085.5	29.2	15.6
Illinois	3,537.9	4,345.6	4,892.0	4,828.2	22.8	12.6
Michigan	2,350.7	3,004.9	3,454.1	3,385.0		14.9
Wisconsin	1,191.9	1,530.4	1,944.8	1,940.0	28.4	27.1
West North Central	3,244.3	5,362.3	6,903.0	6,880.2	65.3	28.7

TABLE 1.5 (continued)

	1960	1970	1980	Dec. 1981[a]	Percent Change 1960-70	Percent Change 1970-80
Minnesota	958.8	1,315.3	1,770.0	1,765.1	37.2	34.6
Iowa	680.1	876.9	1,101.4	1,071.8	28.9	25.6
Missouri	1,350.1	1,668.0	1,969.4	1,966.4	23.5	18.1
North Dakota	126.8	163.6	245.6	253.3	29.0	50.1
South Dakota	142.7	175.4	237.1	235.8	22.9	35.2
Nebraska	384.4	484.3	630.5	634.0	26.0	30.2
Kansas	560.2	678.8	949.0	953.8	21.2	39.8
South						
South Atlantic	7,179.2	10,068.8	14,625.2	14,927.5	40.2	45.3
Delaware	153.9	216.8	258.4	260.3	40.9	19.2
Maryland	896.4[b]	1,349.2	1,695.2	1,696.8	50.5	25.6
Virginia	1,017.6[b]	1,518.9	2,120.9	2,176.9	49.3	39.6
West Virginia	460.0	516.5	645.9	628.0	12.3	25.1
North Carolina	1,195.5	1,782.7	2,385.2	2,393.6	49.1	33.8
South Carolina	582.5	842.0	1,187.4	1,189.7	44.5	41.0
Georgia	1,051.1	1,557.5	2,146.4	2,165.4	48.2	37.8
Florida	1,320.6	2,152.1	3,570.5	3,809.8[c]	62.9	65.9
D.C.	501.6	566.7	615.3	607.0	13.0	8.6
East South Central	2,759.4	3,832.1	5,132.9	5,062.8	38.9	33.9
Kentucky	653.6	910.1	1,209.4	1,187.1	39.2	32.9
Tennessee	925.4	1,327.6	1,734.6	1,706.3	43.5	30.7
Alabama	776.4	1,010.5	1,358.3	1,348.3	30.2	34.4
Mississippi	404.0	583.9	830.6	821.1	44.5	42.3

West South Central	4,267.2	5,957.3	9,313.3	9,874.0	39.6	56.3
Arkansas	367.6	536.2	744.9	742.9	45.9	38.9
Louisiana	783.0	1,033.6	1,571.1	1,652.7	32.0	52.0
Oklahoma	577.1	762.6	1,135.5	1,204.5	32.1	48.9
Texas	2,539.5	3,624.9	5,861.8	6,273.9	42.7	61.7
West						
Mountain	1,874.2	2,665.7	4,468.1	4,612.8	42.2	67.6
Montana	165.0	199.1	280.6	285.1	20.7	40.9
Idaho	155.2	207.8	331.5	323.1	33.9	59.5
Wyoming	96.5	108.3	205.6	214.3	12.2	89.8
Colorado	520.9	750.2	1,251.1	1,298.5	44.0	66.8
New Mexico	236.3	292.6	462.3	469.4	23.8	58.0
Arizona	333.8	547.4	1,003.3	1,033.5	64.0	83.3
Utah	263.1	357.0	554.1	568.1	35.7	55.2
Nevada	103.4	203.3	399.6	420.8	96.6	96.6
Pacific	6,463.8	9,122.9	13,058.8	13,167.1	41.1	43.1
Washington	812.7	1,079.4	1,606.5	1,561.6	32.8	48.8
Oregon	509.7	710.5	1,041.1	990.1	39.4	46.5
California	4,896.0	6,946.2	9,837.6	10,032.4	41.9	41.6
Alaska	56.6	93.1	169.4	176.1	64.5	82.0
Hawaii	188.8	293.7	404.2	406.9	55.6	37.6
U.S. Total	53,059.6	70,286.1	90,814.2	91,679.6	32.5	29.2

[a]Preliminary.
[b]Data not strictly comparable with prior years.
[c]November 1981.
Source: U.S. Department of Labor, Bureau of Labor Statistics, *Employment and Earnings*, various issues.

Between 1970 and 1980, total nonagricultural employment grew 30 percent nationwide but only 20 percent in New England, 6 percent in the Middle Atlantic states, and 15 percent in the East North Central division. The fastest growing division over the ten-year period was the Mountain states at 67 percent, followed by the West South Central division at 56 percent and the South Atlantic states at 45 percent.

A more dramatic interregional shift is observed by focusing on employment changes in manufacturing industries. Manufacturing has been a slow employment growth sector since at least 1965. Indeed, total employment in manufacturing nationwide increased less than 5 percent over the period 1970–81. Thus the growth of manufacturing in one region has usually entailed a decline in another region. Table 1.6 highlights this development.

Since 1950, the Middle Atlantic region has experienced manufacturing job losses of roughly 16 percent. As the data point out, however, most of these losses occurred in the 1970–81 period. Also during this period, the East North Central region began losing manufacturing jobs in large numbers. New York, Illinois, Pennsylvania, Ohio, and New Jersey—the heart of the old manufacturing belt— have suffered the greatest losses in employment, 1,026,712 jobs all told.

While the North has been losing manufacturing jobs, all other areas of the country have been gaining. Since 1950, the Mountain states and the West South Central states have shown the fastest industrial growth. Over the past three decades, Arizona, Nevada, Florida, New Mexico, Texas, Oklahoma, and other Sunbelt states have been transformed into major manufacturing centers. In absolute numbers, Texas is leading all other states in manufacturing job growth since 1970, posting a gain of 366,500.

It would appear that a marked trend toward industrial dispersal from the manufacturing belt has been underway for some time. This loss of manufacturing jobs and industrial plants has been a major factor in the relative economic decline of the Northeast and Midwest. At the same time, manufacturing has become an engine of growth for many areas of the Sunbelt and Mountain states. The causes and consequences of industrial dispersal are discussed in depth in Chapters 4 and 5.

CHANGES IN PERSONAL INCOME

Personal income is perhaps the most comprehensive measure of overall economic performance since it includes income from all sources: manufacturing, services, government, and so forth. A look at changes in per capita personal income since 1950 gives further evidence of economic decline in the industrial North and substantial relative gains throughout much of the Sunbelt (see Table 1.7).

TABLE 1.6
Manufacturing Employment by Region and State,
Selected Years, 1950–81
(In Thousands)

	1950	1970	1981	Percent Change, 1950–81	Percent Change, 1970–81
Northeast					
New England	1,468.6	1,455.6	1,510.3	2.8	3.8
Maine	109.0	110.4	112.8	3.5	2.2
New Hampshire	79.1	91.8	116.4	47.2	26.8
Vermont	36.9	40.5	50.8	37.7	25.4
Massachusetts	715.7	648.3	666.8	− 6.8	2.9
Rhode Island	148.0	120.9	126.3	−14.6	4.5
Connecticut	379.9	443.7	437.2	15.1	− 1.5
Middle Atlantic	4,152.8	4,147.0	3,502.7	−15.7	−15.5
New York	1,915.8	1,760.6	1,432.0	−25.3	−18.7
New Jersey	756.4	863.0	771.0	1.9	−10.7
Pennsylvania	1,480.6	1,523.4	1,299.7	−12.2	−14.7
North Central					
East North Central	4,493.4	5,032.1	4,545.0	1.1	− 9.7
Ohio	1,217.7	1,407.4	1,232.5	1.2	−12.4
Indiana	580.1	710.2	656.9	13.2	− 7.5
Illinois	1,197.9	1,342.1	1,134.9	− 5.2	−15.4
Michigan	1,063.2	1,071.5	977.6	− 8.5	− 8.8
Wisconsin	434.5	500.9	543.1	24.9	8.4
West North Central	874.0	1,226.2	1,342.2	53.6	9.5
Minnesota	200.7	319.4	352.3	75.5	10.3
Iowa	154.4	215.5	235.9	52.8	9.5
Missouri	353.8	446.1	430.0	21.5	− 3.6
North Dakota	6.1	9.9	15.3	150.1	54.5
South Dakota	11.6	15.8	25.8	122.4	63.3
Nebraska	52.1	85.0	95.0	82.3	11.8
Kansas	95.3	134.5	187.9	97.2	39.7
South					
South Atlantic	1,681.8	2,698.2	3,054.2	81.6	13.2
Delaware	51.3	71.2	70.9	38.2	− 0.4
Maryland	232.9	271.1	252.3	8.3	−14.8
Virginia	229.5	365.2	413.0	80.0	13.1
West Virginia	131.4	126.5	111.4	−15.2	−11.9

TABLE 1.6 (continued)

	1950	1970	1981	Percent Change, 1950–81	Percent Change, 1970–81
North Carolina	418.3	718.4	817.3	95.4	13.8
South Carolina	210.4	340.0	388.2	84.5	14.2
Georgia	286.5	465.6	519.9	81.5	11.7
Florida	102.3	321.6	466.5	356.0	45.1
District of Columbia	19.2	18.6	14.7	−23.4	−21.0
East South Central	691.7	1,223.0	1,366.1	97.5	11.7
Kentucky	140.1	252.9	272.1	94.2	7.6
Tennessee	249.9	464.6	506.7	102.8	9.1
Alabama	216.1	323.8	366.0	69.4	13.0
Mississippi	86.4	181.7	221.3	156.1	21.8
West South Central	649.9	1,218.0	1,736.6	167.2	42.6
Arkansas	75.7	167.8	210.3	177.8	25.3
Louisiana	145.0	175.4	220.1	51.8	25.5
Oklahoma	65.6	133.9	198.8	203.0	48.5
Texas	363.6	740.9	1,107.4	204.6	49.5
West					
Mountain	168.4	364.8	573.9	240.8	57.3
Montana	18.0	23.9	23.5	30.5	− 1.7
Idaho	22.4	40.3	52.3	133.5	29.8
Wyoming	6.4	7.4	10.1	57.8	36.5
Colorado	61.6	117.5	184.4	199.4	56.9
New Mexico	10.1	21.0	34.1	237.6	62.4
Arizona	17.0	91.2	159.6	838.8	75.0
Utah	29.4	55.1	89.5	204.4	62.4
Nevada	3.5	8.4	20.4	482.9	142.9
Pacific	1,076.3	2,003.9	2,659.2	147.1	32.7
Washington	178.6	239.4	301.9	69.0	26.1
Oregon	138.0	172.3	203.3	47.3	18.0
California	759.7	1,558.0	2,118.8	178.9	36.0
Alaska	n.a.[a]	8.6	12.0	n.a.	39.5
Hawaii	n.a.	25.6	23.2	n.a.	− 9.4
U.S. Total	15,256.9	19,368.8	20.290.2	33.0	4.8

[a]Not available.

Source: U.S. Department of Labor, Bureau of Labor Statistics, *Employment and Earnings, States and Areas, 1939–74*; *Employment and Earnings*, June 1982.

TABLE 1.7
Per Capita Income by Region and State, Selected Years, 1950–80

	1950	1970	1975	1980	Percent Change 1950–80	Percent Change 1970–80
Northeast						
New England	$1,586	$4,258	$6,080	$10,131	538	138
Maine	1,186	3,272	4,785	7,925	568	142
New Hampshire	1,323	3,745	4,375	9,131	580	144
Vermont	1,121	3,311	4,962	7,827	598	136
Massachusetts	1,633	4,340	6,066	10,125	520	133
Rhode Island	1,605	3,941	5,888	9,444	488	140
Connecticut	1,875	4,871	6,965	11,720	527	141
Middle Atlantic	1,735	4,456	6,411	10,155	485	128
New York	1,873	4,714	6,564	10,260	448	118
New Jersey	1,834	4,635	6,716	10,924	496	136
Pennsylvania	1,541	3,943	5,941	9,434	512	139
North Central						
East North Central	1,675	4,140	6,043	9,802	485	137
Ohio	1,620	3,992	5,832	9,462	484	137
Indiana	1,512	3,752	5,656	8,936	491	138
Illinois	1,825	4,492	6,792	10,521	476	134
Michigan	1,701	4,156	6,169	9,950	485	139
Wisconsin	1,477	3,794	5,674	9,348	533	146
West North Central	1,406	3,746	5,758	9,361	566	150
Minnesota	1,410	3,848	5,817	9,724	590	153
Iowa	1,485	3,749	6,076	9,358	530	150
Missouri	1,431	3,768	5,490	8,982	528	138
North Dakota	1,263	3,120	5,781	8,747	593	180
South Dakota	1,242	3,124	4,924	7,806	529	150
Nebraska	1,490	3,794	6,106	9,365	529	147
Kansas	1,443	3,841	6,046	9,983	592	160
South						
South Atlantic	1,107	3,391	5,517	8,806	695	160
Delaware	2,132	4,483	6,745	10,339	385	131
Maryland	1,602	4,281	6,459	10,460	553	144
Virginia	1,228	3,653	5,786	9,392	665	157
West Virginia	1,065	3,047	4,946	7,800	632	156
North Carolina	1,037	3,218	4,922	7,819	654	143

TABLE 1.7 (continued)

	1950	1970	1975	1980	Percent Change 1950–80	Percent Change 1970–80
South Carolina	893	2,963	4,615	7,266	714	145
Georgia	1,034	3,318	5,072	8,073	681	143
Florida	1,281	3,692	5,640	8,996	602	144
D.C.	2,221	5,333	7,752	12,039	442	126
East South Central	942	2,918	4,692	7,453	691	155
Kentucky	981	3,104	4,886	7,613	676	145
Tennessee	994	3,082	4,909	7,720	677	150
Alabama	880	2,913	4,648	7,488	751	157
Mississippi	755	2,596	4,079	6,580	772	153
West South Central	1,211	3,352	5,321	9,101	652	172
Arkansas	825	2,869	4,617	7,268	781	153
Louisiana	1,120	3,068	4,895	8,458	655	176
Oklahoma	1,143	3,350	5,259	9,116	698	172
Texas	1,349	3,576	5,635	9,545	608	167
West						
Mountain	1,436	3,549	5,501	9,017	528	154
Montana	1,622	3,498	5,433	8,536	426	144
Idaho	1,295	3,280	5,177	8,056	522	146
Wyoming	1,668	3,796	6,079	10,898	553	187
Colorado	1,487	3,839	5,998	10,025	574	161
New Mexico	1,777	3,117	4,768	7,841	566	152
Arizona	1,330	3,631	5,316	8,791	561	142
Utah	1,309	3,228	4,938	7,649	484	137
Nevada	2,018	4,452	6,673	10,727	432	141
Pacific	1,810	4,337	6,494	10,747	494	148
Washington	1,674	4,022	6,284	10,309	516	156
Oregon	1,620	3,694	5,752	9,317	475	152
California	1,852	4,467	6,596	10,938	491	145
Alaska	2,384	4,603	9,535	12,790	436	178
Hawaii	1,386	4,562	6,658	10,101	629	121
U.S. Total	1,496	3,943		9,511		

Sources: U.S. Department of Commerce, Bureau of the Census, *Historical Statistics of the United States*, Ser. F 297–348, 1975, pp. 243–45; *Survey of Current Business*, April 1981, p. 20.

Since 1950, all three census divisions of the industrial North—New England, Middle Atlantic, and East North Central—have shown gains in per capita income below the national average of 535 percent, while all three divisions in the South have grown at rates above the national average. Between 1970 and 1980, per capita income growth in the South Atlantic, East South Central, and West South Central divisions accelerated, posting gains of 155–172 percent compared to a national average of 141 percent. The Middle Atlantic states, at 128 percent, showed the slowest per capita income growth during the 1970–80 period.

Although income convergence among regions appears to be occurring, it is far from complete. While per capita income in the South is growing rapidly, it is still well below that of the Northeast and the nation as a whole. In 1980, thirteen of the sixteen southern states had per capita incomes below the U.S. average. Only Delaware, Maryland, and Texas were above.

The census divisions with above-average income growth since 1970 have all received large numbers of in-migrants. In contrast, the New England, Middle Atlantic, and East North Central divisions, which had below-average income gains, showed heavy out-migration during the 1970–80 period. This suggests that many migrants leaving the North for the Sunbelt have incomes considerably above the national average.

POSTWAR INFLUENCES ON
MIGRATION AND REGIONAL CHANGE

The causes of migration and differential regional development are many and complex. In general, they can be broken down into long-term and short-term factors. Chapter 2 analyzes regional growth and decline as a long-term adjustment to historical and economic forces. In what follows here, a number of recent demographic, environmental, and public policy influences are discussed that may have accelerated the process of regional change.

Interregional Migration of the Armed Forces

The movement of persons entering, leaving, or transferring in the armed forces constitutes an important segment of interregional migration. For a variety of reasons, including the dominance of the Congressional Armed Services Committees by southern politicians and the climatic amenities of the Sunbelt, military installations tend to be concentrated in the lower third of the nation. This predominance of military bases in the South and West has had an appreciable, though not generally recognized, influence on net migration flows among regions.

A recent study of migration patterns within the armed forces[2] found that between 1965 and 1970, a period that coincided with the buildup of the Vietnam

War, military personnel composed 14.2 percent of the interregional migrants. On a net basis, the Northeast and North Central states showed out-migration of military while the South and West states showed substantial in-migration (see Table 1.8). During 1965–70, the loss of population from the North of people entering the armed forces was not compensated for by a gain of in-migrants leaving military service. The total effect of armed forces migration was a loss of 96,225 people from the Northeast and 123,986 people from the North Central region and a net gain of 107,873 in the South and 112,340 in the West.

As a rule, people on active military duty are not making migration decisions

TABLE 1.8
Percentage of Interstate Migrants Entering, Leaving, and Remaining in Armed Forces in Regional Flows, 1965–70

Regional Flow	Entering Armed Forces	Leaving Armed Forces	Remaining in Armed Forces	Total Interstate Migrants
Within Northeast	3.27	4.63	1.89	8.36
North Central to Northeast	2.02	1.84	1.25	2.44
South to Northeast	2.10	9.98	4.42	4.02
West to Northeast	.84	3.93	2.52	1.59
Within North Central	4.11	4.84	2.10	9.90
Northeast to North Central	2.37	2.39	1.39	2.79
South to North Central	2.77	12.16	5.26	6.37
West to North Central	1.08	7.58	3.57	3.57
Within South	18.23	17.01	21.57	17.37
Northeast to South	12.07	3.33	6.00	6.59
North Central to South	15.33	3.61	6.15	7.89
West to South	6.58	7.70	12.88	5.05
Within West	6.17	8.04	8.71	9.77
Northeast to West	4.85	1.98	3.62	2.93
North Central to West	10.09	3.01	4.91	6.02
South to West	8.12	7.98	13.77	5.25
Total Percentage	100.00	100.01	100.01	100.01
Total Numbers	982,581	667,914	325,183	16,990,799

Source: John F. Long, "Interstate Migration of the Armed Forces," paper presented to annual meeting of the Southern Sociological Society, April 1976.

on their own. Such decisions are made by the military authorities, and the individual does not bear the direct costs of the move. However, when leaving the armed forces, individuals are faced with a locational choice that may, in fact, be influenced by their present site:

> There is an economic decision involved in migration upon leaving the armed forces. The migrant's destination is no longer determined by institutional decisions. . . . The move may be back home (to the original place of residence before joining the armed forces), but considerations of moving cost, lack of recent familiarity with the area, intervening opportunities, etc., tend to influence individuals to settle closer to their armed forces residence, other economic conditions being equal.[3]

As mentioned, most of the military installations in the United States are located in the South and West, the two regions that show net gains when all types of military migration during 1965–70 are considered. Presumably, a substantial number of northerners leaving the armed forces were not returning to their states of origin.

Retirees from the armed forces also tend to settle near military installations, in particular to take advantage of PX and medical privileges. California Texas, Virginia, and Florida—the four largest states in terms of military installations—are attracting large numbers of in-migrants (see Table 1.2). Many of them may be military retirees.

Interregional Migration of the Elderly

Because of declining birth rates over the past twenty years, the median age of the U.S. population has been rising. Concomitantly, the number of people aged 65 and over has increased dramatically (see Table 1.9). In 1960, the elderly made up 9.2 percent of the U.S. population. By 1970, the percentage had risen to 9.8,

TABLE 1.9
U.S. Population Aged 65 and Over, Selected Years, 1960–82

1960		1970		1982	
Number	Percent of U.S. Total	Number	Percent of U.S. Total	Number	Percent of U.S. Total
16,559,580	9.2	19,972,330	9.8	26,824,000	11.6

Sources: U.S. Department of Commerce, Bureau of the Census, *Historical Statistics of the United States to 1970*, Ser. A119–134, 1975, p. 15; *Current Population Reports*, Ser. P-25, No. 930, April 1983, p. 2.

and in 1982 persons aged 65 and over accounted for 11.6 percent of the total population. Between 1970 and 1982 alone, the elderly population grew by almost 7 million.

As a result of fifty years of Social Security, Medicare, and post–World War II prosperity, more and more elderly people are able to realize income security during their retirement years. This relative affluence has had the additional effect of encouraging geographical mobility among the elderly, and recent census data suggest that people aged 65 and over are accounting for a growing percentage of total interregional migration.

Between 1970 and 1982, while the elderly population nationwide increased 34.3 percent, the West and South scored gains of 49.2 percent and 48.9 percent in people aged 65 and over (see Table 1.10). By contrast, the elderly popula-

TABLE 1.10
U.S. Population Aged 65 and Over by Region, 1970 and 1982

Region	1970	1982	Increase
Northeast	5,175,626	6,288,000	21.5%
North Central	5,702,667	6,982,000	22.4
South	6,013,590	8,957,000	48.9
West	3,080,447	4,596,000	49.2

Sources: U.S. Department of Commerce, Bureau of the Census, *Historical Statistics of the United States to 1970*, Ser. A119–134, 1975, p. 15; *Current Population Reports*, Ser. P-25, No. 930, April 1983, p. 2.

tion in the Northeast and North Central regions grew by a smaller percentage than the national average. The differential growth patterns are presumably the result of net out-migration of elderly persons from the North.

The apparent preference of the elderly for a southern or western residence can be explained by several factors. A priori, it would be expected that the aged prefer warm climates to cold climates simply because, as a rule, fewer personal inconveniences are encountered in temperate zones. Indeed, a warm or dry climate may be prescribed as a health measure. Second, recent research has determined that current migration by the elderly is strongly influenced through feedback from previous migrants.[4] This flow of "information" helps to reduce the apprehension of potential migrants by providing them with a type of peer group review of the amenities at the new locations.

A third influence on interregional migration by the elderly has been cost-of-living differentials. Since many retirees are on fixed incomes, living costs may be a critical determinant of residential location. Generally, living costs are lower in the South and Southwest than in the North, and this differential has probably helped to lure many retirees to the Sunbelt.

Finally, a number of retirees from the North may be following their children to the Sunbelt. Both a desire to be near family and information flows from sons and daughters about the amenity resources of the South and West may be additional factors influencing interregional migration by the elderly.

Cost-of-Living Differentials

Just as cost considerations have influenced the migration of the elderly, they also can be cited as a general factor attracting economically mobile families to the Sunbelt from the North. As Table 1.11 suggests, there are substantial interregional cost-of-living differentials. For example, in 1981 a family of four at a middle-income budget level required 24 percent more income in the Boston metropolitan area than in Houston to maintain the same standard of living. Recent census data on migration to and from metropolitan areas show that many high-cost areas experienced net out-migration during the 1970–78 period while

TABLE 1.11
Yearly Cost of Living for Family of Four,
Selected Metropolitan Areas, 1981

	Cost of Living			
	Lower Income	Middle Income	Upper Income	Net Migration 1970–78
High-Cost Metropolitan Areas				
Boston, Massachusetts	$16,402	$29,213	$44,821	−73,400
San Francisco–Oakland, California	17,080	27,082	40,006	−40,800
New York–Northeastern New Jersey	15,705	29,540	47,230	−1,051,100
Seattle-Everett, Washington	17,124	25,881	37,396	−18,800
Washington, D.C. Maryland, Virginia	16,702	27,352	41,137	−97,800
Low-Cost Metropolitan Areas				
Houston, Texas	14,810	23,601	34,728	+372,900
Atlanta, Georgia	14,419	23,273	34,623	+117,100
Dallas, Texas	14,392	22,678	33,769	+142,100
Kansas City, Missouri–Kansas	14,925	24,528	36,988	−26,900

Sources: U.S. Department of Commerce, Bureau of the Census, *Current Population Reports*, Ser. P-25, no. 873, February 1980.

low cost areas, located primarily in the Sunbelt, generally had considerable net in-migration.

Over the next several decades it is probable that cost-of-living differentials among regions will narrow significantly.[5] But for the immediate future lower living costs in the Sunbelt will continue to be an inducement to southward migration.

Migration and Environmental Quality

Another contributing factor to the rapid migration to the Sunbelt and Mountain states has been the promise of a better "quality of life" than can be found in other regions of the United States. Although "quality of life" is an imprecise concept, there can be little doubt that the climate, the open space, the economic opportunities, and a relaxed life style have helped to attract large numbers of people and businesses to these areas.

Paul Schwind has suggested that an "unseen hand" of climatic preference is operating to guide a large proportion of both individuals and footloose industries toward locations that are well endowed with nonexportable amenity resources, in particular year-round warm temperatures.[6] Recent census data would seem to confirm such a preference. Of the twenty-two fastest-growing metropolitan areas between 1970 and 1980, six were in Florida, four were in Texas, three were in California, and two were in Arizona.[7]

A study by David Morgan also reveals an inherent preference among many Americans for living environments rich in nonexportable amenities, especially the Sunbelt and the Mountain states.[8] Working through the National Opinion Research Center at the University of Chicago, Morgan conducted a nationwide sample survey during 1973-74 from which he was able to ascertain whether or not the respondent desired to live in a state other than the one of current residence. As Table 1.12 indicates, a considerably larger proportion of repondents in the Middle Atlantic, East North Central, and West North Central census divisions wished to change residence than was the case among respondents in the South and West. Indeed, the only section of the North where respondents were less anxious to move out of the region than the national average was New England.

Morgan was also able to determine from his questionnaire the particular census division to which the respondent would move if given a choice. Figure 1.3 indicates the changes in population distribution by region that would occur if everyone desiring to live elsewhere moved to the region of preference. The largest increase, 124 percent, would occur in the Mountain states, followed by a 41 percent increase in the Pacific division. The South Atlantic states would show an 11 percent increase, while the West South Central division would grow by 1.3 percent. The MIddle Atlantic, East North Central, and West North Cen-

TABLE 1.12
Rank Order of Regions by Proportion Desiring to Live Elsewhere
(Intraregional Migrants Excluded)

Region	Proportion
Middle Atlantic	.308
East North Central	.302
West North Central	.292
New England	.209
East South Central	.171
West South Central	.171
South Atlantic	.140
Mountain	.137
Pacific	.128
United States as a whole	.224

Source: David J. Morgan, *Patterns of Population Distribution: a Residential Preference Model and its Dynamic* (Chicago: University of Chicago Department of Geography, 1976).

tral regions would lose 27 percent, 25 percent, and 21 percent of their populations if everyone desiring to live elsewhere could move to the region of preference.

Migration trends since 1970 seem to conform to the preferences expressed in the Morgan survey (see Table 1.2). The census division actually showing the highest net in-migration rate, the Mountain states, is the area that would show the largest relative population gain as a result of population redistribution based on preferences. The Pacific and South Atlantic states registered high rates of in-migration as well. Indeed, all of the regions predicted to grow on the basis of Morgan's data have shown heavy net in-migration since 1970. Similarly, the large population losses predicted for the Middle Atlantic and East North Central divisions seem to be occurring. Between 1970 and 1980, the Middle Atlantic states lost 1,946,000 persons as a result of net out-migration while the East North Central states lost 1,324,000.

To reiterate, the concepts of "quality of life" and "environmental quality" are quite subjective and difficult to quantify. Yet they are clearly a strong influence on migration decisions, either intrametropolitan or interregional. The amenities (quality of life) of the rapidly growing Southern and Western regions—less environmental degradation, more moderate climates, ease of communication, availability of recreational resources, lower crime rates, and so on—are apparently striking a responsive chord with many residents of the older, congested areas of the Northeast and Midwest.

FIGURE 1.3
**Proportional Changes in Population by Region if Everyone Desiring to
Live Elsewhere Moved to the Region of Preference**

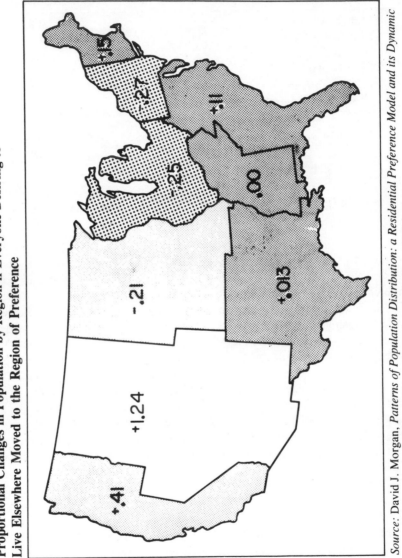

Source: David J. Morgan, *Patterns of Population Distribution: a Residential Preference Model and its Dynamic* (Chicago: University of Chicago Department of Geography, 1976).

The Distribution and Impact of Federal Spending

Much of the ongoing public debate about regional growth and decline has focused on the differential impacts of federal tax and spending policies. It has been alleged by many northern politicians that favorable federal spending policies have been instrumental in bringing about the rapid growth of the Sunbelt while accelerating the decline of the industrial North. Such assertions are often backed up by statistical computations showing that the Northeast and Midwest states are running "balance-of-payments" deficits with the federal government— that they are sending more to Washington in the form of taxes than they are receiving in federal outlays. For example, a study by the Northeast-Midwest Institute calculated that "the states of the Northeast and Midwest sent $165 billion more in taxes to Washington than they got back in federal spending," while states in the South and West, on the other hand, ran sizeable "balance-of-payments" surpluses.[9]

But as Table 1.13 indicates, the Southwest and Rocky Mountain states, as well as those of the Mideast and Great Lakes, all show spending/taxation ratios less than one on a per capita basis. Of course such ratios do not, by themselves, either support or refute northern claims of regional discrimination. Indeed, an

TABLE 1.13
Federal Government Spending and Taxes per Capita by Region, Fiscal Year 1982

Region	Federal Spending per Capita	Federal Taxes per Capita	Spending/ Taxes Ratio
New England	$3,089	$3,044	1.01
Mideast	2,745	3,427	0.80
Great Lakes	1,984	2,976	0.66
Plains	2,461	1,900	1.30
Southeast	2,538	1,725	1.47
Southwest	2,350	3,022	0.78
Rocky Mountain	2,416	2,626	0.92
Far West	3,001	2,708	1.11
U.S. Total	2,573	2,573	

Note: Regions in this table are roughly comparable to those regional definitions used in Chapter 2. See Table 2.2.

Sources: U.S. Department of Commerce, Bureau of the Census, *Federal Expenditures by State for Fiscal Year 1982; Report of the Commissioner of the Internal Revenue Service, Fiscal Year 1982.*

a priori expectation of regional balances between spending and taxes would totally ignore the significant distributional aspects of federal fiscal policy.

The distributional impact of federal tax and spending policies has been summarized by C.L. Jusenius and L.C. Ledebur:

> One of the functions of fiscal policy is to redistribute income among groups according to goals determined by society. One of these redistributive goals, however well met, has been to close the gap between "the rich" and "the poor." In part, the federal government has attempted to meet this goal through the federal income tax system: taxpayers with higher income levels also pay relatively higher proportions of their incomes in taxes. On the expenditures side, public policy has been directed toward raising the real income of the lowest socioeconomic groups. Fiscal policy also serves to redistribute income among geographic regions. [10]

As can be seen in Table 1.7, per capita income in the South Atlantic, East South Central, West South Central, and Mountain divisions is well below the national average, while the New England, Middle Atlantic, and North Central divisions show per capita incomes above the national average. Thus it is not surprising that the average tax payment per person is lower in the South and Mountain states than it is in the North. The tax differentials simply reflect the relative income positions of the regions.

Though growing rapidly, the South is still the poorest region of the nation. Yet there is no evidence that overall federal spending levels in the South exceeded the national average of $2,573 in 1982. Per capita spending in 1982 came to $2,538 in the Southeast and $2,350 in the Southwest (see Table 1.13). Per capita spending in both New England and the Mideast, on the other hand, significantly exceeded the national average.

State-by-state or region-by-region comparisons of federal taxes and expenditures are misleading on other grounds as well. For example, a number of federal spending programs are channeled to persons rather than local governments or private contractors. Social Security payments, federal retirement, military pensions, and welfare payments are received by individuals who are highly mobile. The fact that many retirees are moving to the Sunbelt, and bringing their Social Security or federal retirement checks with them, is not a matter of discretionary fiscal policy.

Furthermore, state-by-state comparison of federal spending does not reveal any significant patterns of favoritism toward the Sunbelt. Table 1.14 presents per capita federal outlays by state in 1976 and 1980 for five major spending categories: defense contracts, defense salaries, retirement programs, welfare, and highways and sewers. Only in the case of defense salaries do the southern and western states generally show higher per capita spending levels. Taking into account the fact that the preponderance of military installations is situated in the South and West, this result is to be expected.

TABLE 1.14
Per Capita Federal Outlays in Five Categories

State	Per Capita 1976	Per Capita 1980	Percent Change 1976–80
		Defense Contracts[a]	
Northeast			
New England:			
Maine	$ 270.96	$ 413.17	52.5
New Hampshire	199.89	358.42	79.3
Vermont	276.47	246.03	−11.0
Massachusetts	346.61	666.26	92.2
Rhode Island	114.08	277.35	143.1
Connecticut	622.46	1248.86	100.6
Middle Atlantic:			
New York	185.99	328.61	76.7
New Jersey	146.55	223.44	52.5
Pennsylvania	159.28	243.01	52.6
North Central			
East North Central:			
Ohio	114.34	192.33	68.2
Indiana	160.83	246.00	53.0
Illinois	56.79	98.68	73.8
Michigan	111.75	190.26	70.3
Wisconsin	57.48	81.09	41.1
West North Central:			
Minnesota	178.92	265.11	48.2
Iowa	88.95	104.54	17.5
Missouri	512.43	673.95	31.5
North Dakota	329.47	146.63	−55.5
South Dakota	49.30	42.63	−13.5
Nebraska	45.72	106.25	132.4
Kansas	161.55	351.68	117.7
South			
South Atlantic:			
Delaware	64.85	419.10	546.3
Maryland	280.16	518.87	85.2
Virginia	385.00	744.62	93.4
West Virginia	60.98	66.24	8.6
North Carolina	79.78	121.39	52.2

TABLE 1.14 (continued)

State	Per Capita 1976	Per Capita 1980	Percent Change 1976–80
South Carolina	83.22	148.84	78.9
Georgia	129.23	199.81	54.6
Florida	139.13	227.81	63.6
District of Columbia	1559.59	2262.98	45.1
East South Central:			
Kentucky	86.27	88.40	2.5
Tennessee	91.12	119.15	30.8
Alabama	153.54	237.90	54.9
Mississippi	438.34	332.52	−24.1
West South Central:			
Arkansas	75.70	85.92	13.5
Louisiana	133.43	184.94	38.6
Oklahoma	155.73	204.01	31.0
Texas	197.84	420.38	112.5
West			
Mountain:			
Montana	103.05	51.93	−50.0
Idaho	58.76	35.99	−39.0
Wyoming	84.58	80.80	−4.4
Colorado	171.59	209.68	22.2
New Mexico	145.55	253.85	74.4
Arizona	304.76	307.95	1.0
Utah	172.49	213.65	23.9
Nevada	61.32	80.55	31.4
Pacific:			
Washington	416.75	622.07	49.3
Oregon	48.17	77.54	61.0
California	446.25	611.11	36.9
Alaska	588.02	757.66	28.8
Hawaii	494.38	400.26	−19.0
U.S. Total	213.24	332.48	55.9
	Defense Salaries[b]		
Northeast			
New England:			
Maine	82.83	144.39	74.3
New Hampshire	210.62	286.35	35.9

TABLE 1.14 (continued)

State	Per Capita 1976	Per Capita 1980	Percent Change 1976–80
Vermont	39.81	50.84	27.7
Massachusetts	58.04	84.91	46.3
Rhode Island	162.03	188.58	16.4
Connecticut	38.94	91.96	136.2
Middle Atlantic:			
New York	31.97	45.68	42.9
New Jersey	85.53	118.47	38.5
Pennsylvania	75.80	105.24	38.8
North Central			
East North Central:			
Ohio	66.94	91.74	37.0
Indiana	61.74	74.91	21.3
Illinois	63.57	86.96	36.8
Michigan	35.67	47.76	33.9
Wisconsin	19.10	28.77	50.6
West North Central:			
Minnesota	28.59	39.05	36.6
Iowa	18.40	25.78	40.1
Missouri	126.62	148.05	17.9
North Dakota	269.79	307.73	14.1
South Dakota	143.16	200.92	40.3
Nebraska	133.62	202.09	51.2
Kansas	170.25	201.73	18.5
South			
South Atlantic:			
Delaware	167.20	214.61	28.4
Maryland	284.24	347.62	22.3
Virginia	461.88	755.58	63.6
West Virginia	21.25	32.20	51.5
North Carolina	206.34	232.04	12.5
South Carolina	292.25	381.80	30.6
Georgia	213.28	275.14	29.0
Florida	139.62	187.23	34.1
District of Columbia	850.39	1235.94	45.3
East South Central:			
Kentucky	195.93	203.74	4.0
Tennessee	60.76	74.98	23.4

TABLE 1.14 (continued)

State	Per Capita 1976	Per Capita 1980	Percent Change 1976–80
Alabama	173.72	238.18	37.1
Mississippi	155.81	216.30	38.8
West South Central:			
Arkansas	94.34	120.26	27.5
Louisiana	105.21	124.66	18.5
Oklahoma	260.88	290.67	11.4
Texas	205.71	213.83	3.9
West			
Mountain:			
Montana	131.77	136.35	3.5
Idaho	106.85	131.02	22.6
Wyoming	171.20	173.88	1.6
Colorado	275.10	261.50	−5.0
New Mexico	265.43	342.55	29.1
Arizona	188.34	203.92	8.3
Utah	306.28	361.49	18.0
Nevada	225.76	250.64	11.0
Pacific:			
Washington	239.12	285.64	19.5
Oregon	34.46	47.05	36.5
California	200.26	260.29	30.0
Alaska	873.89	1066.46	22.0
Hawaii	850.46	1217.82	43.2
U.S. Total	139.17	182.33	31.0
	Retirement Programs[c]		
Northeast			
New England:			
Maine	499.76	618.40	23.7
New Hampshire	496.24	715.10	44.1
Vermont	450.07	658.45	46.3
Massachusetts	455.19	706.80	55.3
Rhode Island	523.28	797.84	52.5
Connecticut	411.47	655.84	59.4
Middle Atlantic:			
New York	442.03	691.40	56.4
New Jersey	439.30	694.73	58.1

TABLE 1.14 (continued)

State	Per Capita 1976	Per Capita 1980	Percent Change 1976–80
Pennsylvania	483.67	762.38	57.6
North Central			
East North Central:			
Ohio	410.68	635.59	54.8
Indiana	392.56	625.02	59.2
Illinois	406.07	609.19	50.0
Michigan	389.45	600.63	54.2
Wisconsin	424.25	651.22	53.5
West North Central:			
Minnesota	411.16	611.75	48.8
Iowa	425.11	670.77	58.8
Missouri	485.34	728.36	50.1
North Dakota	398.65	612.28	53.6
South Dakota	433.06	670.38	54.8
Nebraska	455.42	696.77	53.0
Kansas	486.50	706.55	45.2
South			
South Atlantic:			
Delaware	413.22	667.14	61.4
Maryland	433.34	692.54	59.8
Virginia	521.50	785.07	50.5
West Virginia	517.13	734.92	42.1
North Carolina	384.81	600.94	56.2
South Carolina	394.49	607.37	54.0
Georgia	409.52	604.61	47.6
Florida	658.89	1010.33	53.3
District of Columbia	991.47	1686.20	70.1
East South Central:			
Kentucky	401.38	624.53	55.6
Tennessee	417.72	621.02	48.7
Alabama	443.05	677.05	52.8
Mississippi	407.34	616.00	51.2
West South Central:			
Arkansas	499.49	759.37	52.0
Louisiana	364.35	530.03	45.5
Oklahoma	498.80	711.31	42.6
Texas	410.22	578.42	41.0

TABLE 1.14 (continued)

State	Per Capita 1976	Per Capita 1980	Percent Change 1976–80
West			
Mountain:			
Montana	451.13	694.12	53.9
Idaho	429.09	627.61	46.3
Wyoming	416.42	525.89	26.3
Colorado	424.96	612.35	44.1
New Mexico	433.21	667.05	54.0
Arizona	519.36	780.72	50.3
Utah	391.61	552.61	41.1
Nevada	445.10	656.37	47.5
Pacific:			
Washington	516.15	723.44	40.2
Oregon	506.14	715.97	41.5
California	448.70	638.30	42.3
Alaska	223.29	352.32	57.8
Hawaii	393.72	635.53	61.4
U.S. Total	454.81	675.80	48.6

	Welfare[d]		
Northeast			
New England:			
Maine	151.34	207.21	36.9
New Hampshire	83.58	110.33	32.0
Vermont	158.07	201.67	27.6
Massachusetts	152.32	199.28	30.8
Rhode Island	147.19	212.97	44.7
Connecticut	81.73	129.22	58.1
Middle Atlantic:			
New York	158.02	271.15	71.6
New Jersey	107.35	145.24	35.3
Pennsylvania	106.63	158.48	48.6
North Central			
East North Central:			
Ohio	97.79	134.45	37.5
Indiana	66.43	104.02	56.6
Illinois	113.39	149.62	32.0

TABLE 1.14 (continued)

State	Per Capita 1976	Per Capita 1980	Percent Change 1976–80
Michigan	116.44	183.01	57.2
Wisconsin	114.45	169.85	48.4
West North Central:			
Minnesota	103.03	146.16	41.9
Iowa	81.34	112.18	37.9
Missouri	94.84	127.81	34.8
North Dakota	69.40	100.85	45.3
South Dakota	79.57	127.81	60.6
Nebraska	68.56	89.01	29.8
Kansas	75.42	98.03	30.0
South			
South Atlantic:			
Delaware	87.19	128.28	47.1
Maryland	102.20	134.55	32.6
Virginia	77.41	115.76	49.5
West Virginia	116.06	155.82	34.3
North Carolina	111.49	145.92	30.9
South Carolina	126.78	180.05	42.0
Georgia	127.12	171.06	34.6
Florida	92.75	116.19	25.3
District of Columbia	256.49	356.64	39.0
East South Central:			
Kentucky	153.41	193.68	26.2
Tennessee	127.90	180.45	41.1
Alabama	126.99	187.83	47.9
Mississippi	156.83	213.10	35.9
West South Central:			
Arkansas	158.58	201.49	27.1
Louisiana	157.56	209.50	33.0
Oklahoma	112.36	153.25	36.4
Texas	96.37	118.12	22.6
West			
Mountain:			
Montana	77.99	112.51	44.3
Idaho	73.35	109.40	49.1
Wyoming	47.51	50.41	6.1

TABLE 1.14 (continued)

State	Per Capita 1976	Per Capita 1980	Percent Change 1976–80
Colorado	93.83	94.44	1.0
New Mexico	128.12	164.88	28.7
Arizona	60.08[e]	65.84[e]	9.6
Utah	69.29	94.39	36.2
Nevada	79.09	76.79	−2.9
Pacific:			
Washington	111.14	129.60	16.6
Oregon	107.22	123.98	15.6
California	150.52	173.71	15.4
Alaska	84.53	198.85	135.2
Hawaii	138.58	178.55	28.8
U.S. Total	120.49	163.60	35.8

	Highways and Sewers[f]		
Northeast			
New England:			
Maine	94.10	65.89	−30.0
New Hampshire	75.42	86.68	14.9
Vermont	65.20	90.42	38.7
Massachusetts	22.73	36.30	59.7
Rhode Island	49.90	58.64	17.5
Connecticut	59.87	48.88	−18.4
Middle Atlantic:			
New York	32.50	54.26	67.0
New Jersey	76.71	45.77	−40.3
Pennsylvania	35.71	56.55	58.4
North Central			
East North Central:			
Ohio	41.82	45.42	8.6
Indiana	25.95	56.36	117.2
Illinois	41.31	46.85	13.4
Michigan	30.99	51.46	66.1
Wisconsin	31.08	46.53	49.7
West North Central:			
Minnesota	53.19	56.90	7.0
Iowa	62.86	70.91	12.8

TABLE 1.14 (continued)

State	Per Capita 1976	Per Capita 1980	Percent Change 1976–80
Missouri	53.62	63.06	17.6
North Dakota	67.50	122.05	80.8
South Dakota	70.49	103.46	46.8
Nebraska	37.56	71.82	91.2
Kansas	34.59	83.79	142.3
South			
South Atlantic			
Delaware	64.98	80.08	23.2
Maryland	34.67	143.63	314.3
Virginia	85.65	50.87	40.6
West Virginia	55.73	151.10	171.1
North Carolina	29.16	42.57	46.0
South Carolina	44.74	30.08	−32.8
Georgia	37.39	70.45	88.4
Florida	36.95	62.22	68.4
District of Columbia	108.79	214.26	96.9
East South Central:			
Kentucky	37.68	78.70	108.9
Tennessee	36.90	47.70	29.3
Alabama	40.18	70.01	74.2
Mississippi	29.50	40.40	36.9
West South Central:			
Arkansas	56.61	50.63	−10.6
Louisiana	64.20	56.18	−12.5
Oklahoma	35.23	48.13	36.6
Texas	30.62	49.52	61.7
West			
Mountain:			
Montana	128.99	140.38	8.8
Idaho	42.82	61.94	44.7
Wyoming	95.69	164.24	71.6
Colorado	46.05	65.21	41.6
New Mexico	48.16	54.99	14.2
Arizona	34.13	53.25	56.0
Utah	57.12	78.25	37.0
Nevada	128.47	124.40	−3.2

TABLE 1.14 (continued)

State	Per Capita 1976	Per Capita 1980	Percent Change 1976–80
Pacific:			
Washington	41.31	117.79	185.1
Oregon	48.85	65.99	35.1
California	34.98	43.47	24.3
Alaska	248.14	307.80	24.0
Hawaii	68.12	95.40	40.0
U.S. Total	42.89	59.30	38.3

[a]Includes civil functions prime contracts, military prime construction contracts, military research & development RDTE contracts, military prime service contracts, military prime supply contracts, and prime contracts of less than $10,000.

[b]Includes civilian pay, military active duty pay, and military reserve and National Guard pay.

[c]Includes military retired pay, Social Security disability, retirement insurance and survivors insurance, Civil Service retirement and disability fund, railroad retirement, and Veteran's Administration disability compensation and pensions.

[d]Includes food stamps, assistance payments and maintenance assistance, medical assistance program, supplemental security income, and unemployment insurance.

[e]Does not include Medicaid.

[f]Includes highway planning and construction funds and construction grants for wastewater treatment works.

Sources: U.S. Department of Commerce, Community Services Administration, *Geographic Distribution of Federal Funds in Summary*, Fiscal Year 1976 and Fiscal Year 1980.

In the area of defense contracts, some states within each region show spending levels above the national average of $332 per capita in 1980 while others are below. Only in the Pacific division is defense contracting systematically above the national level. Again, this result is not surprising given the presence of Boeing, Hughes Aircraft, Northrop Corporation, Rockwell International, and the Aerojet-General Corporation in the Pacific states. It should also be noted that data on defense contracts by state relate only to primary contractors. All major defense-oriented companies subcontract with other firms throughout the country, but no adjustment is made in the federal spending figures. For example, in 1980 California received $15 billion in primary defense contracts; but probably only a fraction of this amount was actually spent within the state.

In the case of welfare spending, both the Northeast and the South contain states that are receiving above-average payments. These states all have high proportions of their populations at poverty levels. Above-average retirement pay-

immigration from Europe.
rrived in the United States
n growth in those three de-
) fully three-quarters of the

rstate migration after 1870.
g outside their state of birth
vere living in states noncon-
er of studies have suggested
between 1870 and 1900 was
ountry to the cities. Accord-

s in the West for urban as
al urban centers within the
nal migration declined, and
fects of the cityward move-
after 1870, large numbers of
moved to the rapidly urbaniz-
-born residents also left the
es were compensated for by

cter of the U.S. population in
proportion of native-born white
tain regions, not surprisingly,
ive to those regions. Table 2.1
cks from the Deep South had
ercent of the black population

tion relates to the large flow of
s outflow peaked in the 1940s
eached 49.3 per 1,000 popula-
t black out-migration from the
ple so that by 1960, 26 percent
the South.
ons in U.S. history has been the
e areas where they were living
emselves and their families else-
pioneers, the southern blacks in
income whites who led the surge
has been defined as "one form
stribution of opportunities and

ments are generally found in states with large proportions of retirees, such as Florida, Arizona, and the District of Columbia.

CONCLUSION

This chapter has documented the nature of regional growth and decline in the United States since 1950. Over the past thirty years, the South and West regions of the United States have shown dramatic population gains while the Northeast and North Central regions have grown only moderately. Much of the population gains in the South and West has resulted from net in-migration from the Northeast and North Central regions. As a result of these migration trends, employment and per capita personal income are rising faster in the southern and western states than is the case in the Northeast and North Central regions.

Northern politicians have recently pointed to regional favoritism in federal spending as the major cause of Sunbelt prosperity and northern decline. However, these claims are not supported by available data on federal outlays by state.

In any case, the importance of federal spending to the economic development of the Sunbelt has been much overstated. The North has been losing people, jobs, and investment to the Southeast and Southwest for nearly three decades. To a large extent, the migration of population and employment opportunities is occurring in response to economic forces affecting the cost and efficiency of production. Lower living costs, taxes, energy costs, and land costs in many parts of the Sunbelt have facilitated the economic development of the region but at the same time have improved the overall efficiency and productivity of the national economy.

Economic growth in the Sunbelt has become self-sustaining as a result of growing markets and a broadening industrial base. Given the present diversity and dynamism of the Sunbelt's economy, it is unlikely that a redirection of federal funds to the North would stem the flow of people, investment, and jobs to the region.

NOTES

1. See Table 1.2 in this chapter.
2. John F. Long, "Interstate Migration of the Armed Forces," paper presented to annual meeting of the Southern Sociological Society, April 1976.
3. Long, "Interstate Migration."
4. Steve L. Barsby and Dennis R. Cox, *Interstate Migration of the Elderly* (Lexington, Mass.: Lexington Books, 1975), 41–52.
5. See discussion in Chapter 2.
6. Paul J. Schwind, *Migration and Regional Development in the United States, 1950–1960*, Department of Geography Research, Paper No. 133 (Chicago: University of Chicago, 1971), 114.

7. U.S. Department of Commerce, Bureau of the Census, *1980 Cens* 51–5, October 1981.

8. David J. Morgan, *Patterns of Population Distribution: A Residenti its Dynamic* (Chicago: University of Chicago Department of Geography,

9. Northeast-Midwest Institute, *The State of the Region 1981* (Washi Midwest Institute, 1981), 37.

10. C.L. Jusenius and L.C. Ledebur, *A Myth in the Making: The Soutl and Northern Economic Decline* (Washington, D.C.: Economic Developi search Report, 1976), 28.

This was also the period of virtually unrestricted Between 1890 and 1920, 18.2 million immigrants a and accounted for 42 percent of the overall populatic cades. Most immigrants settled in cities, and in 192 foreign-born population were urban residents.[4]

Census data indicate a decline in the rate of inte By 1900, the proportion of native-born people livin had decreased to 21 percent, and only 11 percent v tiguous to their states of birth.[5] However, a numbe that the decline in the volume of interstate migration related to an increase in local migration from the c ing to David Ward:

> It would appear that before about 1870 opportuniti
> well as agricultural employment competed with loc
> areas of distance movements within the total inter
> even newly settled areas began to experience the ef
> ment. . . . Although interstate migration diminishes
> native-born residents from the North Central states r
> ing Western and Southwestern states. Many native
> Northeastern and Southeastern states, but these loss
> gains in internal migration.[6]

Table 2.1 illustrates the highly mobile chara 1920. The Middle Atlantic region had the highest residents—94.3 percent. In the Pacific and Mour only about one-half of the 1920 residents were na also shows that in 1920 the out-migration of bla not yet assumed major dimensions. Only 16 pe resided outside the southern states in 1920.

The third significant phase of internal migra blacks out of the South from 1920 to 1960. Th when net migration for blacks from the South r tion aged 25 to 44. Between 1920 and 1960 ne sixteen southern states exceeded 3.5 million pec of the nation's black population resided outside

A common thread to all of the mass migrati search for economic opportunity. People left t because they perceived better opportunities for t where. This was true of the nineteenth-century the 1920s and 1940s, and the educated, middle- to the Sunbelt in the 1970s. Indeed, migration of human response to the uneven spatial di resources."[7]

TABLE 2.1
White and Nonwhite Population by Region

	1920 Population (white)	Percent Native Born	1920 Population (nonwhite)	Percent Native Born
Northeast	5,420,554	92.3	68,704	53.5
Middle Atlantic	16,651,261	94.3	562,963	41.8
East North Central	17,641,695	88.5	522,270	36.4
West North Central	10,798,750	80.6	311,204	62.5
South Atlantic	9,311,926	91.1	4,315,975	98.0
East South Central	6,286,445	92.1	2,516,980	95.3
West South Central	7,615,242	76.1	2,110,266	88.5
Mountain	2,730,830	52.8	105,563	73.6
Pacific	4,264,922	48.4	109,913	66.4

Source: U.S. Department of Commerce, Bureau of the Census, *Historical Statistics of the United States,* 1975, Ser. C15—24.

The major difference between the contemporary southward migration and previous mass migrations is that, whereas total population was growing rapidly during earlier periods of regional change, population growth has now slowed to a trickle. Because birth rates and death rates are relatively stable now, internal migration is the major determinant of changes in population distribution.

Natural increase and immigration from abroad are no longer offsetting population losses due to internal migration in some regions. Since 1970 annual population growth, including legal immigration from other countries, has averaged about 0.8 percent. Therefore a number of states in the Middle Atlantic and East North Central regions are showing absolute population losses for the first time. Between 1972 and 1983, the following states lost population: Rhode Island, New York, Pennsylvania, Ohio, and the District of Columbia. The Northeast region as a whole, composed of the New England and Middle Atlantic States, has a smaller population now than it did in 1972.[8]

Obviously, there is a strong relationship between migration and regional economic development. As Simon Kuznets has pointed out:

> Since economic growth is measured primarily as an increase in output, and since internal migration toward greater earning opportunities is also migration toward greater production opportunities, such internal migration is partly responsible for economic growth; without it some of the economic growth that was realized would not have been possible.[9]

Migration also affects personal income, employment, and the demand for public services in both growing and declining areas. Typically, states receiving large numbers of migrants show per capita income growth above the national average while those states losing population show slower-than-average income growth.[10] Rapidly growing regions offen require heavy public expenditures for roads, schools, and utilities while declining regions find themselves faced with the heavy public outlays for unemployment, welfare, and other social services.

Much of the recent debate on regional growth and decline in the United States has focused on federal spending and other public policies that have allegedly "favored" certain regions or states at the expense of others. No doubt, federal fiscal flows have had some impact on regional development, and these effects are discussed in Chapter 1. But regional growth and decline can be better understood in the context of structural change within a dynamic economic system—that system being the United States as a whole.

Economists and regional scientists have been much concerned with regional development and adjustment in recent decades. In what follows, a number of regional growth theories are reviewed that may help to explain the post-1950 regional growth and decline in the United States.[11]

THE STAGES-OF-GROWTH MODEL

Early attempts to explain the economic development process in terms of growth stages were made by a number of German economists, such as F. List, B. Hildebrand, K. Bucher, and G. Schmoller, in the late nineteenth century. But probably the best known, and most useful, of the growth-stage views of economic development is that posited by W.W. Rostow.[12] Although Rostow is concerned mainly with the economic growth process in less-developed countries, his analysis seems to have some relevance for contemporary regional growth in the United States, and especially the emergence of the Sunbelt South.

In Rostow's model, the economic history of any society can be differentiated into five stages: (1) traditional, (2) preconditions for takeoff, (3) takeoff, (4) drive to maturity, and (5) mass consumption. The first, or traditional, stage refers to a society characterized by limited technology and a rigid, hierarchical social structure. The southern United States prior to World War I might fit such a description.

During the second, or pretakeoff, stage, both the society's economic and its social structure begin to change. As investment is increased in the transportation and communications infrastructure, traditional agriculture becomes mechanized, and raw resources are exploited, a new social and political elite evolves. Indeed, many southern and western states exhibited such changes during the interwar period. The completion of the federal highway system, the construction of dams and reservoirs throughout the South, the mechanization of farming, and the huge investment in the petroleum industry in the Southwest helped set the stage for an economic takeoff.

According to Rostow, the third, or takeoff, stage occurs when "the forces making for economic progress . . . expand and come to dominate the society. Growth becomes its normal condition."[13] But the takeoff stage must be initiated by some sort of external stimulus that is followed by a steady increase in the rate of productive investment, the development of a substantial manufacturing sector, and the emergence of a political, social, and institutional framework that encourages continued growth.[14]

Historically, the prod to takeoff has been a particularly sharp stimulus such as political revolution that has directly affected the balance of social power or a technological innovation that has set in motion a chain of expansion to spawn a modern, industrialized economy. In the case of the U.S. South, the stimulus was World War II.

During the war, billions of defense dollars and millions of military personnel poured into the southern states. As Kirkpatrick Sale has commented:

This is a region that was transformed, and brought into modernity, by World War II, when the defense establishment moved in to take advantage of its benign climate, vast open spaces, extensive and for the most part protected coastline, abundant and cheap labor, and nascent shipping and aircraft industries, altogether pumping in an estimated 60 percent of its $74 billion wartime expenditures into these fifteen states. And as the defense installations and contractors continued to grow with growing defense budgets even after the war, they continued to build up the substructure of the whole economy, in practically every state from North Carolina to California.[15]

An important legacy from World War II was the implantation of many high technology industries throughout the South, especially in aerospace and electronics. The rise of these industries fostered the rapid takeoff of manufacturing, which remains the primary engine of economic growth in the Sunbelt today. As for the requisite political, social, and institutional change for economic takeoff, the South since World War II has clearly met the test. Racial integration, political moderation, and a favorable business climate have all helped to accelerate the pace of economic growth in the region.[16]

The takeoff stage, according to Rostow, lasts twenty to thirty years. Thus the South may now be making the transition to the fourth, or maturing, stage:

After take-off there follows a long interval of sustained if fluctuating progress as the now regularly growing economy drives to extend modern technology over the whole front of its economic activity. . . . The make-up of the economy changes increasingly as technique improves, new industries accelerate, older industries level off. . . . Goods formerly imported are produced at home, new import requirements develop, and new export commodities to match them.[17]

Certainly, the economy of the South is increasingly diversified. In a recent study, William Miernyk ascertained that whereas there were major differences between the structure of the nation and the South in 1940, by 1975 most of these differences had disappeared.

In 1940, employment in agriculture in the South was 73 percent above the national average. The proportion of workers in the production of basic energy was also about one-third larger than the national average. In all other major sectors, however, the South had below-average levels of employment. By 1975, the proportion of agricultural workers in the South was exactly equal to the national average. Manufacturing employment still lagged behind the nation, but only by 10 percent. The percentages of southern workers in transportation, communications, utilities, and government were above national averages. In the remaining sectors—except for basic energy and construction—differences in the structure of employment in the South and in the nation were small or negligible.[18]

These structural changes suggest that import substitution is occurring throughout the South and that the South is also developing export markets, both domestically and internationally, for its manufactures and services.

Rostow's stages-of-growth model of economic development has been roundly criticized by economists, historians, and regional scientists for lacking precision, inner logic, and empirical validation.[19] Nonetheless, the pattern of economic development of the southern United States since World War I seems to conform well to Rostow's model.

THE EXPORT BASE MODEL

Several economists have stressed the role of exports in regional economic development.[20] In its simplest form, export base theory asserts that the regional growth rate is a function of regional export performance.

> This ability to export induces a flow of income into the region which, through the familiar multiplier effect, tends to expand the internal markets of the region for both national and region-serving goods and services. . . . As the regional market expands and region-serving activities proliferate, conditions may develop for self-reinforcing and self-sustaining regional growth, and new internal factors may become important in determining the rates of regional growth, such as external economies, associated with social overhead capital and the agglomeration of industries, and internal economies of scale.[21]

The resource endowments of a particular region determine its comparative advantage in the national economy. Whether or not that region will grow, however, is determined by the demand patterns of the nation as a whole. For example, the Appalachian region has a clear-cut export advantage in the production of coal, but, until very recently, the region was stagnating because of a lack of sufficient domestic and foreign demand for the resource. Resource endowments include services and amenities as well as natural resources, and over time a region's endowments may be modified through technological change, economic reorganization, importation of capital, or changes in the quantity and quality of the labor force.

Export-producing industries are critical to regional growth for several reasons. First, they attract income from other regions, often bringing about a balance-of-payments surplus. This surplus may in turn be used to finance imports of other goods and services. Second, export industries tend to be technologically advanced and to operate at comparatively high levels of productivity. Income generation from high-productivity industries filters through the region and helps to spur the development of residentiary (nonexport) industries. Third, export industries generally have strong forward and backward linkages with other regions and industries, and this encourages the integration of the developing region with the national economy. Finally, a strong export sector permits a region to shift part of its tax burden to residents of other areas.

Historically, the development of most regions in the United States can be explained in terms of an export base. In the preindustrial United States, the South specialized in and exported agricultural commodities, while the North engaged in light manufacturing and financial services. Between 1870 and 1950, the Northeast-Midwest manufacturing belt achieved rapid economic development by producing and exporting finished goods to all other regions of the nation.

The recent development of the Sunbelt and Mountain states also can be viewed with reference to export base theory. In large part, the rapid growth of Texas, Louisiana, Oklahoma, and other energy-endowed states has resulted from a large and growing national demand for energy products. Although energy production by itself does not account for much in the way of employment, the oil and gas industries have strong linkages with other industries.[22] Not surprisingly, chemicals, iron and steel, transportation, and utilities are fast-growing industries in the Southwest. Tertiary activities, such as banking, real estate, and professional services, have also sprung up in support of the energy (export) sector.

"Amenity" resources have also served as an export base for much of the Sunbelt and Mountain regions. Americans tend to be heliocentric, and the increasing demand for travel and recreation has meant a growing export market for regional amenity resources in such places as Florida, California, Texas, Arizona, and the Rocky Mountain states. Quality of life has also been marketed by many Sunbelt and Mountain states as a lure to people and industry.

Harvey Perloff and Lowdon Wingo have pointed out that while exports of resource products provide the basis for regional economic development, extensive and continued growth can be expected to take place only in those regions that achieve sizeable internal markets.[23] The Sunbelt, as a result of massive inmigration over the past two decades, would seem to have crossed that threshold. Growth has become self-sustaining as the region's industrial base has broadened and deepened.

Export base theory may also offer some clues to understanding the relative decline of the Northeast in the national economy. In short, the region may be suffering from what Jean Fourastie has called "tertiary crisis"—that is, more people employed in tertiary activities than its primary and secondary sectors can support.[24]

In a recent study, William Miernyk summarized the debate regarding the role of the tertiary sector in regional economic development as follows:

> In the late 1940's, Hyson and Neal argued that if the momentum of regional economic development is to be maintained there must be a progressive shift of the labor force from the secondary to the tertiary sector. The late Seymour Harris questioned this. He felt that a region can become too dependent on trade and service activities. A rising proportion of tertiary employment, he argued, does not always reflect an increasing standard of living. . . . It may also reflect a deterioration in manufacturing, or a loss of a region's earlier comparative ad-

vantage. The same view has been advanced by Jean Fourastie who stated that a shift in the labor force from the secondary to the tertiary sector which is not the result of technological progress is evidence of growing economic weakness rather than increased economic strength. A region does not have a high per capita income because it has a large tertiary sector; rather, as the real income of a region increases, it can afford to have a progressively larger proportion of its labor force engaged in trade and service activities. If the economy of a region shifts too rapidly from secondary to tertiary activities...the result will be a relative decline rather than an increase in per capita income.[25]

Why has relative income been declining in the Northeast for some time? The region has been losing manufacturing (secondary) jobs for forty years. Since substantial employment growth was occurring in the tertiary sector, especially trade and government, the conventional wisdom suggested that manufacturing job losses did not matter. In fact, the region was losing its basic export industries and substituting local service industries with a much narrower economic and tax base.

REGIONAL INCOME INEQUALITY MODELS

A number of economic development theories can be broadly encompassed under the rubric of regional income inequality models. Again, many of these theories were framed with a view toward explaining the economic growth process in the developing nations. But they also appear to shed some light on the process of regional growth and decline in the United States.

Factor Price Equalization

The notion of factor price equalization over time emerged from the Hecksher-Ohlin theory of international/interregional trade and integration.[26] The critical assumption of this theory is that factors of production—labor, capital, and so on—are free to move along the economic landscape to seek their "opportunity costs" or highest return. Eventually, an equilibrium is reached where returns to factors, or income, are equalized among regions. In short, this theory suggests that any differences in income levels among regions are temporary and will disappear over time.

Differential growth rates in per capita income over the past half century suggest that factor price equalization is, indeed, occurring among the regions of the United States (see Table 2.2 and Figure 2.1). In 1929, per capita income in the Southeast was only 53 percent of the U.S. average and 38 percent of the Mideast average. Per capita income in South Carolina, the lowest state in 1929, was only 23 percent that of New York, the highest state. By 1981, per capita income in

TABLE 2.2
Per Capita Personal Income in Dollar Amount and as Percentage of U.S. Average by Region and State, Selected Years, 1929-81

Region and State[a]	Per Capita Personal Income 1981	Per Capita Personal Income as Percentage of U.S. Average						Percentage Point Change 1929-81
		1981	1976	1964	1954	1944	1929	
U.S. Average[b]	$10,517	—	100	100	100	100	100	—
New England	10,333	98.3	97	98	99	101	112	− 13.7
Maine	8,655	82.3	84	83	79	91	85	− 2.7
New Hampshire	10,073	95.8	93	92	92	88	98	− 2.2
Vermont	8,654	82.3	85	82	78	78	89	− 6.7
Massachusetts	11,158	106.1	102	109	106	109	130	− 23.9
Rhode Island	10,466	99.5	101	102	105	106	124	− 24.5
Connecticut	12,995	123.6	114	125	129	134	146	− 22.4
Mideast	11,705	111.3	113	117	120	122	141	− 29.7
New York	11,400	108.7	110	122	121	129	165	− 56.3
New Jersey	12,115	115.2	113	120	125	131	132	− 16.8
Pennsylvania	10,373	98.6	100	101	101	104	110	− 11.4
Delaware	11,279	107.2	113	123	130	124	145	− 37.8
Maryland	11,534	109.7	109	107	106	111	111	− 1.3
District of Columbia	13,487	128.2	134	131	136	131	181	− 52.8
Great Lakes	10,514	100.0	104	105	108	107	109	− 9.0
Michigan	11,009	104.7	109	109	114	116	113	− 8.3
Ohio	10,371	98.6	100	103	110	111	111	− 12.4

Indiana	9,656	91.8	97	99	101	100	87	+4.8
Illinois	11,479	109.1	115	117	121	117	136	+26.9
Wisconsin	10,056	95.6	98	97	96	93	97	−1.4
Plains	10,179	96.8	92	88	90	87	76	+20.8
Minnesota	10,747	102.2	96	92	94	84	85	+17.2
Iowa	10,149	96.5	100	93	97	82	82	+14.5
Missouri	9,876	93.9	93	96	96	90	89	+4.9
North Dakota	10,525	100.1	84	78	70	84	53	+47.1
South Dakota	8,793	83.6	74	71	78	80	59	+24.6
Nebraska	10,296	97.9	97	90	94	90	84	+13.9
Kansas	10,870	102.4	101	96	99	97	76	+26.4
Southeast	8,714	82.9	84	74	69	67	53	+29.9
Virginia	10,445	99.3	97	88	84	75	62	+37.3
West Virginia	8,334	79.2	84	75	69	69	66	+13.2
Kentucky	8,455	80.4	84	74	71	64	56	+24.4
Tennessee	8,604	81.8	84	87	68	72	54	+27.8
North Carolina	8,679	82.5	84	75	69	64	48	+34.5
South Carolina	8,050	76.5	80	67	63	61	38	+38.5
Georgia	8,960	85.3	86	73	71	70	50	+35.3
Florida	10,050	95.6	95	87	85	91	74	+21.6
Alabama	8,200	78.0	79	71	62	62	46	+32.0
Mississippi	7,256	69.0	71	59	51	53	41	+28.0
Louisiana	9,468	90.0	84	76	75	74	59	+31.0
Arkansas	8,042	76.5	79	69	58	56	43	+33.5
Southwest	9,825	93.4	89	84	85	81	69	+24.4
Oklahoma	10,210	97.1	88	83	81	79	65	+32.1

TABLE 2.2 (continued)

Region and State[a]	Per Capita Personal Income 1981	Per Capita Personal Income as Percentage of U.S. Average						Percentage Point Change 1929–81
		1981	1976	1964	1954	1944	1929	
Texas	10,743	102.1	97	87	90	87	68	+34.1
New Mexico	8,654	82.3	81	79	79	73	58	+24.3
Arizona	9,693	92.2	90	87	91	87	84	+ 8.2
Rocky Mountain	9,962	94.7	93	90	93	94	84	+10.7
Montana	9,676	92.0	87	87	97	98	85	+ 7.0
Idaho	8,906	84.7	89	83	84	90	72	+12.7
Wyoming	11,780	112.0	104	95	102	103	96	+16.0
Colorado	11,142	105.9	101	97	96	89	91	+14.9
Utah	8,307	79.0	85	88	87	89	80	– 1.0
Far West[c]	11,706	111.3	107	111	118	126	117	– 5.7
Washington	11,266	107.1	105	106	112	129	107	– 0.1
Oregon	9,991	95.0	98	99	102	119	97	– 2.0
Nevada	11,633	110.6	114	120	137	124	125	–14.4
California	12,057	114.6	111	120	122	132	142	–27.4
Alaska	14,190	134.9	158	116	129	–	–	n.a.[d]
Hawaii	11,096	105.5	108	108	101	104	–	n.a.[d]

[a]Divisional totals are unweighted averages.
[b]Includes Alaska and Hawaii in 1981, 1976, and 1964 but not in earlier years.
[c]Regional total excludes Alaska and Hawaii.
[d]Not available.
Source: U.S. Department of Commerce, Bureau of the Census (Washington, D.C.: U.S. G.P.O., 1975).

FIGURE 2.1

Per Capita Personal Income as Percentage of U.S. Average by Region, 1929–2000 (projected)

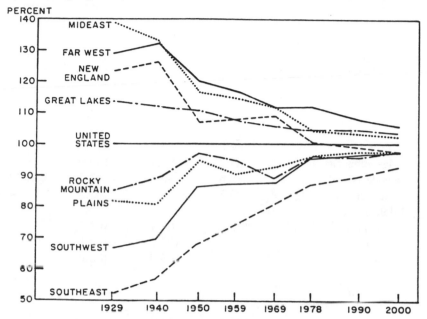

Source: U.S. Department of Commerce, Bureau of Economic Analysis. Figure drawn by cartography lab at Syracuse University.

the Southeast had reached 83 percent of the U.S. average and 74 percent of the Mideast average. Per capita income in Mississippi, the lowest state in 1981, was 62 percent of that in Illinois, one of the highest states (excluding Alaska).

With the exception of Indiana, all of the states of the Northeast-Midwest manufacturing belt showed relative declines in per capita income between 1929 and 1981, and in some cases, such as New Jersey, Delaware, and New York, the declines were dramatic. In contrast, all of the southeastern and southwestern states posted substantial gains in relative per capita income. The southeastern and southwestern states have also been the largest recipients of immigrants in recent years, suggesting that these individuals are, in fact, migrating in search of their "opportunity costs," and thereby bringing about income convergence among regions.

A similar pattern can be discerned by looking at relative changes in manufacturing wages over time, especially with reference to the states in the Northeast-Midwest manufacturing belt (see Table 2.3). Many of these states showed relative declines in manufacturing wages between 1951 and 1981. Any increases in

TABLE 2.3
Average Hourly Earnings of Production Workers on
Manufacturing Payrolls by Region and State, 1951, 1976 and 1981

Region and State	Index of Average Hourly Earnings			Change, 1951–81
	1981	1976	1951	
Northeast				
New England				
Maine	86.6	80.8	87.3	− 0.7
New Hampshire	85.3	82.1	89.3	− 4.0
Vermont	89.8	85.0	88.7	+ 1.1
Massachusetts	89.7[a]	91.7	100.0	−10.3
Rhode Island	80.6	80.4	93.3	−12.7
Connecticut	100.5	98.7	105.3	− 4.8
Middle Atlantic				
New York	102.2	102.1	108.7	− 6.5
New Jersey	103.6	103.3	109.3	− 5.7
Pennsylvania	106.2	103.3	106.0	+ 0.2
North Central				
East North Central				
Ohio	123.4	117.3	122.0[b]	+ 1.4[b]
Indiana	121.1	115.8	114.0	+ 7.1
Illinois	114.9	111.3	111.3	+ 3.6
Michigan	138.7	130.2	124.0	+14.7
Wisconsin	115.8	108.1	108.1	+ 7.7
West North Central				
Minnesota	110.7	105.2	103.3	+ 7.4
Iowa	120.1	111.9	103.3	+16.8
Missouri	103.8	99.8	100.0	+ 3.8
North Dakota	91.3	91.9	115.3[c]	−24.0
South Dakota	87.7	85.6	90.0	− 2.3
Nebraska	104.0	94.8	92.0	+12.0
Kansas	106.1	96.0	105.3	+ 0.8
South				
South Atlantic				
Delaware	108.4	103.8	102.0	+ 6.4
Maryland	106.8	107.3	98.0	+ 8.8
District of Columbia	112.8	105.6	n.a.[d]	n.a.[d]
Virginia	89.8	83.3	84.7	+ 5.1
West Virginia	111.3	105.8	105.3	+ 6.0

TABLE 2.3 (continued)

Region and State	Index of Average Hourly Earnings			Change, 1951–81
	1981	1976	1951	
North Carolina	77.7	73.7	78.7	− 1.0
South Carolina	81.3	76.3	79.3	+ 2.0
Georgia	82.8	80.4	77.3	+ 5.5
Florida	85.2	84.4	78.0	+ 7.2
East South Central				
Kentucky	103.7	99.0	110.7e	− 7.0e
Tennessee	87.1	81.2	86.0	+ 1.1
Alabama	89.5	86.5	84.7	+ 4.8
Mississippi	79.2	72.9	68.7	+10.5
West South Central				
Arkansas	81.6	75.6	72.7	+ 8.9
Louisiana	115.4	103.7	89.3	+26.1
Oklahoma	105.8	91.5	98.7	+ 7.1
Texas	104.2	95.4	98.7	+ 5.5
West				
Mountain				
Montana	119.1	118.1	116.7	+ 2.4
Idaho	101.1	106.3	112.7	−11.6
Wyoming	104.1	108.5	122.0	−17.9
Colorado	102.8	103.3	103.3	− 0.5
New Mexico	89.3	77.7	96.0	− 6.7
Arizona	107.6	99.8	106.7	+ 0.9
Utah	100.7	79.6	104.0	− 3.3
Nevada	110.6	112.3	119.3	− 8.7
Pacific				
Washington	135.9	123.5	124.7	+11.2
Oregon	123.2	119.0	129.3	− 6.1
California	112.8	108.5	118.0	− 5.2
Alaska	161.0	161.7	n.a.	n.a.
Hawaii	98.4	90.2	n.a.	n.a.

aPercentage uses April 1981 figures.
bData are not available for 1951; index is computed for 1952 earnings.
cIndex is based on 1956 earnings.
dNot available.
eIndex is based on 1954 earnings.
Source: U.S. Department of Labor, Bureau of Labor Statistics, *Employment and Earnings, States and Areas, 1939–1974,* 1975, and *Employment and Earnings,* June 1982.

relative wages can probably be explained by the predominance of the highly un-
ionized and capital-intensive industries in those states.

Most of the Sunbelt states have shown substantial relative gains in manufacturing earnings. In part, these relative wage gains are a reflection of changes in
the Sunbelt's industrial mix. Historically, the region's economy was dominated
by labor-intensive, low-wage industries such as textiles, apparel, wood products,
and food processing. Indeed, as late as 1976 nearly 42 percent of the South's
manufacturing employment was in low-wage industries, compared to only 20 percent for the United States.[27] In recent years, however, higher-wage, capital-
intensive manufacturing, such as electronics, aerospace, and instruments, has
spread across the Sunbelt, helping to pull up average earnings. The explosion
of energy prices during the late 1970s also helped drive up manufacturing wages
in those Sunbelt states producing and processing oil, gas, and coal.

In Table 2.4, changes in average hourly earnings for two low-wage industries (textiles and apparel) and two high-wage industries (fabricated metals and
machinery) are compared over time for four northern states (New Hampshire,
Massachusetts, New York, and Pennsylvania) and four southern states (North
Carolina, South Carolina, Tennessee, and Texas). In the low-wage industries,
the four southern states generally show relative increases in average hourly earnings between 1958 and 1980, whereas the pattern is mixed for the four northern states. In the high-wage industries, three of the four southern states show
a trend of relative wage increases, while the northern industrialized states ex-
hibit a downward trend in relative wages.

Though not as strong an indication as per capita income convergence, trends
in manufacturing wages over the past thirty years would seem to reinforce the
notion that interregional factor price equalization is taking place in the United
States.

Unbalanced Growth Theories

The two names most frequently associated with unbalanced growth theories
are Gunnar Myrdal and Albert Hirschman.[28] Both view economic development
as a seesaw process between leading and lagging regions. While significant divergence in growth rates and incomes among regions is expected during the early
periods of development, in the long run both Myrdal and Hirschman predict a
movement toward interregional equilibrium.

Myrdal's theory of unbalanced growth is centered around the notion of "cumulative causation." He argues that market forces will tend to draw economic
activity toward certain areas that possess an initial comparative advantage based
on location, transportation infrastructure, or some other attribute. The build-up
becomes self-sustaining due to increasing internal and external economies with
the result that little investment or growth occurs outside the emerging region.
The lagging areas are further debilitated by what Myrdal calls "backwash

effects." Skilled workers, entrepreneurs, and capital migrate to the rapidly growing regions to seek higher returns. Goods and services produced in the growing regions inundate the lagging areas and inhibit the development of indigenous enterprise. The level of public services, such as health and education, is likely to be inferior in the lagging regions. Thus these backwash effects reinforce the tendency for interregional divergence as development proceeds.

However, a second set of residual forces, known as "spread effects," may actually help to stimulate growth in the lagging regions. Expansion in the economic center may generate a demand for agricultural products and raw resources from the depressed areas with the result that income and investment flow into these regions. If the spread effects are stronger than the backwash effects, the process of cumulative causation will lead to the development of new economic centers.

Such situations are most likely to occur in countries that already have achieved a fairly high level of economic development since this "is accompanied by improved transportation and communications, higher levels of education, and a more dynamic communion of ideas and values—all of which tends to strengthen the forces for the centrifugal spread of economic expansion or to remove the obstacles for its operation."[29] Also, in more developed countries, spread effects are likely to be accompanied by public policies intended to spur the development of lagging regions.

Hirschman's model of growth is quite similar to Myrdal's though it is not based on a cumulative causation hypothesis. Rather, the emphasis is on the transmission of growth from rapidly expanding metropolitan centers to lagging or depressed hinterlands.

Hirschman assumes that development occurs initially around one or more regional centers of economic strength:

> This need for the emergence of "growing points" or "growth poles" in the course of the development process means that international and interregional inequality of growth is an inevitable concomitant and condition of growth itself. Thus, in the geographical sense, growth is necessarily unbalanced.[30]

But once growth takes a firm hold in one region, it sets in motion counterbalancing forces that tend to pull up lagging regions over time. These forces he calls "trickling down" and "polarization" effects, which are nearly analogous to Myrdal's spread and backwash effects.

In describing the growth transmission process, Hirschman uses the terms "North" and "South" to define the expanding and lagging regions:

> The growth of the North will have a number of direct economic repercussions on the South, some favorable, others adverse. The favorable effects consist of the trickling down of Northern progress: by far the most important of these effects is the increase of Northern purchases and investments in the South, an in-

TABLE 2.4
Average Hourly Earnings in Selected Industries and States,
1958 and 1980 (National Average = 100)

State	Index/Avg. Hr. Earn. 1980	Index/Avg. Hr. Earn. 1958	Change, 1958–80	Index/Avg. Hr. Earn. 1980	Index/Avg. Hr. Earn. 1958	Change, 1958–80
	SIC 22, Textiles			SIC 23, Apparel		
New Hampshire	98.0	101.3	− 3.3	96.3	86.4	+ 9.9
Massachusetts	105.5	108.7	− 3.2	108.5	99.4	+ 9.1
New York	85.6	116.8	−31.2	118.2	124.7	− 6.5
Pennsylvania	98.6	106.7	− 8.1	104.4	95.5	+ 8.9
North Carolina	97.4	94.6	+ 2.8	89.7	77.3	+12.4
South Carolina	104.9	96.0	+ 8.9	89.1	74.0	+15.1
Tennessee	95.9	91.9	+ 4.0	94.5	n.a.[a]	n.a.
Texas	100.0	88.6	+11.4	89.3	81.2	+ 8.1

	SIC 34, Fabricated Metals			SIC 35, Machinery Exc. Electrical		
New Hampshire	79.9	73.3	+ 6.6	77.8	n.a.	n.a.
Massachusetts	92.5	n.a.	n.a.	86.1	96.6	−10.5
New York	78.8	99.6	−20.8	103.4	99.6	+ 3.8
Pennsylvania	103.6	104.4	− 0.8	101.5	100.8	+ 0.7
North Carolina	83.9	73.8	+10.1	74.9	66.7	+ 8.2
South Carolina	76.8b	70.2c	+ 6.6	71.5b	60.8	+10.7
Tennessee	87.0d	87.1d	− 0.1	75.5d	87.7d	−12.2
Texas	96.9	92.0	+ 4.9	91.6	90.3	+ 1.3

aNot available.
bData for SIC 34 and 35 were aggregated for South Carolina.
cIndex based on 1962 data.
dData for SIC 35 and 36 were aggregated for Tennessee.

Source: U.S. Department of Labor, Bureau of Labor Statistics, *Employment and Earnings, States and Areas, 1939–74,* 1981.

crease that is sure to take place if the economies of the two regions are at all complementary. In addition, the North may absorb some of the disguised unemployed of the South and thereby raise the marginal productivity of labor and per capita consumption in the South.

On the other hand, several unfavorable or polarization effects are also likely to be at work. Comparatively inefficient, yet income-creating, Southern activities in manufacturing and exports may become depressed as a result of Northern competition. . . . Northern progress may denude the South of its key technicians and managers as well as of the more enterprising young men. This type of migration may actually be undesirable not only from the point of view of the South but also from that of the country as a whole, for the loss to the South due to the departure of these men may be higher than the gain to the North.[31]

In the case where the trickle-down effects outweigh the polarization effects, market forces will tend to restore an equilibrium among the competing regions. If not, Hirschman suggests, public investments will be channeled to depressed areas.

Although Myrdal and Hirschman did not have the United States in mind when referring to northern (growing) and southern (lagging) regions, their description of the economic growth process sounds remarkably like the U.S. experience over the past century. Prior to 1880, no particular region dominated the U.S. economy, and manufacturing was spread widely across the country. But between 1880 and 1910, the Northeast and Midwest emerged as the dominant industrialized region of the nation and came to be known as the "manufacturing belt." As late as 1937, these seventeen states contained 72 percent of all manufacturing activity in the United States (see Figure 2.2).

How did this one region come to dominate the national economy? To use Myrdal's terms, the region possessed "initial advantages" that attracted and fostered economic development. The dense railroad network of the North provided the region with access to raw materials and markets. Growing demands for iron and steel, coupled with cost-saving technological advantages, allowed producers in the manufacturing belt to produce more cheaply than their counterparts in other regions (Myrdal's backwash effect). Another important factor in the concentration of industry in this region was its proximity to coal deposits, which were then the principal source of energy for the United States and a key input for the production of steel.

But spread or trickle-down effects also emanated from the industrial core. Northern capital was invested in the South and West to improve transportation, to develop agriculture, and especially to generate the raw material requirements for the great industries of the manufacturing belt. Indeed, the resource endowments of the South and West, developed with northern capital, would become the basis for the eventual economic expansion of those regions. In addition, the North absorbed millions of migrants, especially blacks, from the South, which may have helped to increase the marginal productivity of labor and per capita income in that region.

FIGURE 2.2
U.S. Manufacturing Belt, 1937

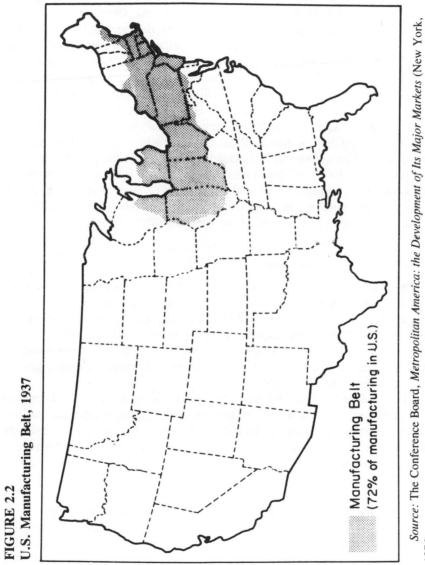

Manufacturing Belt
(72% of manufacturing in U.S.)

Source: The Conference Board, *Metropolitan America: the Development of Its Major Markets* (New York, 1976).

During and after World War II, the spread effects from the North became even more pronounced. Improvements in communications and transportation helped to reduce spatial barriers to the transmission of growth impulses. The South became more accessible to the North, both as a source of raw materials and as a market for northern products and investments. Obsolescence of physical plant, increased congestion, and environmental degradation in the manufacturing belt also have spurred the gradual relocation of people and economic activity to the South and Southwest during the post–World War II period.

Both Myrdal and Hirschman observed that spread or trickle-down effects could be encouraged by governmental policies intended to spur growth in lagging regions. Since at least the 1930s, the U.S. federal government has pursued such a course. The Tennessee Valley Authority, the Area Redevelopment Administration, and the Appalachian Regional Commission are but a few examples of massive public investment in the southern states over the past few decades.

By the mid-1960s, the South had emerged as a new locus of self-sustained economic growth. Moreover, Myrdal's process of cumulative causation, in conjunction with natural market forces, is spurring the South toward income convergence with the other regions of the United States.

Losch's Economic Landscape

Similar in its assumptions, but somewhat different in its implications, is the notion of the economic landscape posited by August Losch.[32] Losch, building on the earlier work of Hecksher and Ohlin, argued that comparative advantage, through which a region may experience economic development, is inherently spatially dynamic. That is, ever-changing market forces, and hence ever-changing opportunities, cause comparative advantages to shift constantly among alternative locations on the landscape.

In the short term, the location of economic activity on the landscape appears relatively static as producers and consumers proceed about the business of satisfying their immediate needs and wants. Over the long term, however, the economic landscape is characterized by considerable change: the breakup of established combinations of factors of production and patterns of economic activity due to vanished opportunities and the creation of new arrangements in response to new opportunities.

This schema seems to characterize the recent decline of the Northeast and emergence of the Sunbelt. As the opportunities that initially spawned the enterprises of the old manufacturing belt vanished and traditional industries became increasingly unprofitable, economic activity—population, jobs and income—was attracted to new opportunities and comparatively more profitable ventures in the South. Unlike the factor price equalization and unbalanced growth theories, however, Losch's conception of a dynamic economic landscape does not provide for eventual income equalization among regions. Indeed, Losch's view of eocnomic development is much like that of Joseph Schumpeter: an economy constantly in dynamic disequilibrium, characterized by incessant structural change (see discussion below). Such a vision, of course, suggests that the forces that have transformed the Northeast will eventually come to play in the Sunbelt as well.

A SCHUMPETERIAN PERSPECTIVE ON REGIONAL GROWTH AND DECLINE

Joseph Schumpeter's schema of the capitalist development process may shed some additional light on the phenomena of regional growth and decline in the United States.[33]

In Schumpeter's view, the process of economic development emerges from the fiercely competitive environment of the capitalist system. This competitive struggle he called "creative destruction." Capitalism grows by destroying old economic structures and creating new ones. Old firms and products are driven out of business by more efficient and innovative producers.

In the Schumpeterian analysis of the development process, the key figure is the entrepreneur. It is the entrepreneur who adapts to the risks and uncertainties of the capitalist system and who recognizes or seeks out new investment and product opportunities.

> The function of entrepreneurs is to reform or revolutionize the pattern of production by exploiting an invention or, more generally, an untried technological possibility for producing a new commodity or producing an old one in a new way, by opening up a new source of supply of materials or a new outlet for products, by reorganizing an industry and so on.[34]

Schumpeter predicted that the very success of capitalism would sow the seeds of its eventual demise for three reasons. First, capitalism would erode its own institutional framework by destroying its protective strata of gentry, small-business owners and farmers, and by seriously weakening individual proprietorship in favor of the modern corporation. Second, the entrepreneurial function would become obsolete. Technological progress and innovation would fall into the hands of research and development specialists and thereby become routinized and bureaucratized. Third, the capitalist system would generate growing social hostility among intellectuals and laborers, which would lead to a decomposition of the political framework on which capitalism rests.

What has all this to do with the rise of the Sunbelt and the decline of the Northeast? Schumpeter did not have a spatial context in mind when discussing the process of creative destruction, yet it is easy to visualize the Sunbelt and the Northeast as rising and declining systems of entrepreneurial capitalism. For a variety of reasons, related to age of development and slow population growth, the social and political framework on which capitalism so critically depends seems to have diminished in the Northeast. At the same time, the entrepreneurial spirit appears to be alive and well throughout much of the South. Sunbelters have not yet succumbed to the lofty, postindustrial attitudes that prevail in the North. Money making, trade, sales ability, and economic expansion have a positive connotation. Opportunities for financial aggrandizement and the application of entrepreneurial acumen have helped to attract risk takers to the region.

Similarly, the politically conservative environment of most southern states reinforces the institutional setting for competitive capitalism. Taxes are low, and labor unions are generally weak. The near absence of union influence reflects both a deep cultural bias against them and the existence of restrictive labor legislation. In the Northeast, by contrast, Schumpeter's predictions of social hostility to capitalism may have been realized. High taxes on people and business, liberal social welfare legislation, strong union pressures, and the coalescence of organized interest groups have stifled the atmosphere in which competitive capitalism can survive.

To use Mancur Olson's phrase, "institutional arthritis" has retarded the rate of economic growth in the Northeast, while the Sunbelt has not yet been afflicted with the disease.[35] This is perhaps most apparent in the proliferation of books, articles, and proposals for legislation touting a "national industrial policy" as a "solution" to the regional problems caused by the structural changes that are transforming the national economy.[36] Although some differences are to be found among the various "national industrial policy" proposals, all are premised on the notion that structural changes, and the accompanying regional dislocations of people and property, are crises that require some form of interventionist remedy. Too, all of the proposals for a "national industrial policy" have spatial and hence regional implications. Some, of course, are more explicit than others in that they would place controls on plant location and even restrictions on plant closings.[37] Others, while not as explicitly spatial, would have a profound impact at the local and regional level through the allocation of federal money to specific "targeted" growth industries, or the subsidization and protection of declining industries.[38] Ultimately, all of the "national industrial policy" proposals seek to either freeze, delay, or in some way mitigate the effects of structural change and regional growth and decline.

Industry and Regional Life Cycles

The idea that economic activity is spatially dynamic has been formally and explicitly developed in product and regional life cycle theories.[39] Specifically, these theories hold that, over time, innovations introduced in a particular industry find export markets as incomes abroad rise and as labor costs at home increase. Thus exports from the industry tend to grow, setting a pattern that might be termed the "new product" stage. In time, however, new influences come to bear on the established trade pattern: (1) the demand in some export markets grows sufficiently large to support local production that can exploit the existing scale economies and (2) the product becomes sufficiently standardized that price competition begins to play an important role. Considerations of the cost of factors of production acquire a spatial dimension, a pattern that might be termed the "maturing product" stage. During this stage, as lower factor costs tip the scale in favor of alternative locations for sales outside the producing region, competitors are likely to appear. Eventually, the output of competing regions may become price competitive in the domestic market of the original producer, so that a region formerly exporting a particular commodity may find itself importing. This final phase of the product cycle may be termed the "standardized product" stage.

The product cycle theory has an explicitly spatial dimension as each phase of the cycle has different locational requirements. The new product stage, which is characterized by innovation and, hence, a comparatively high input of research and development, usually occurs in high-cost regions. The standardized product stage, on the other hand, favors lower-cost regions. Indeed, this phenomenon helps explain the substantial loss of jobs from the traditional manufacturing belt during the postwar years. Moreover, and in the same vein as Myrdal's notion of "cumulative causation," as the decentralization of production occurs, receiving regions will tend to develop economies of scale. In conjunction with an increasing demand in the region for the product, scale economics may stimulate indigenous entrepreneurial potential. Evidence of this phenomenon can be seen in the emergence of new industrial growth centers in the Sunbelt.[40] In other words, regions over time may change their roles from that of recipients of innovation to that of generators of innovation.

This, in turn, suggests the presence of regional life cycles that build upon Nikolai Kondratieff's long waves and Schumpeter's notion of "creative destruction." That is, new economic enterprises in new regions bypass existing enterprises in older regions that have become obsolete and increasingly unprofitable.[41] Too, this notion may be thought of as an elaboration of Losch's conception of an economic landscape characterized by a migration of economic activity that *does not* necessarily result in equilibrium. Indeed, the notion of a regional life cycle strongly suggests that the Sunbelt will inevitably experience a decline as well, as comparative advantage shifts to other locations on the landscape.

A REGIONAL TAXONOMY

The previous discussion of unbalanced growth has focused on the *process* of development—the centripetal and centrifugal forces of cumulative causation, spread effects, polarization, and so on. Therefore, regions, and their attendant stages of development, can be viewed as the *result* of the growth process.

Myrdal and Hirschman speak generally about "growing" and "lagging" regions but do not specify their structure in much detail. A more definitive taxonomy can be found in the work of John Friedmann.[42] Friedmann distinguishes five basic regions that exist at any stage of national (or international) economic development: core regions, upward transitional areas, resource frontier zones, downward transitional areas,and special problem areas.[43]

Core regions are those subsystems of an economy already at an advanced stage of development and characterized by a high capacity for generating innovation. Historically, the manufacturing belt has been the core region of the United States, but since World War II a second core region has emerged—California. According to Friedmann, the chief problems affecting core regions include sustaining growth, organizing a livable physical environment, and managing a complex metropolitan society. Clearly, these problems are manifest today in the United States' core regions.

In recent years, the manufacturing belt has not been able to sustain the industrial growth and technological innovations that enabled it to dominate the national economy for many decades. Many sections of the manufacturing belt are suffering from environmental degradation and social disorganization as well. California, while still showing strong economic growth, is nonetheless beset by serious erosion of its quality of life due to congestion and pollution.

Upward transitional areas are settled regions with strong commercial relations to core regions. They are areas of rapid economic development characterized by large influxes of people and capital from both the core regions and rural areas. Typically, they are less concentrated and less urbanized than core regions. The problems facing upward transitional areas are those generally encountered by rapidly growing regions: urbanization, industrialization, and transportation.

The Sunbelt is obviously the dominant upward transitional area in the United States today. As mentioned earlier, this region has been the major recipient of population and industrial growth over the past decade. And the critical problems facing the Sunbelt today are those of managing rapid economic development.

Resource frontier zones are areas of new settlement with low population densities and potentials for new growth based on raw resource exports. Problems encountered in these areas typically include the building of transportation and communication infrastructures, the need for large-scale investments in agriculture, mining, or forestry, and the extension of basic administrative and social services. The Mountain states, along with Alaska, constitute the resource frontier of the United States today, especially with regard to the development of energy resources.

Downward transitional areas are old, established regions characterized by declining economies and an out-migration of people and industry. An aging and obsolete industrial plant is often coupled with high rates of unemployment and few possibilities for new development. These areas are adjusting to a lower and less intensive level of economic activity in an effort to redefine their relationship to the national economic system.

A number of urban centers in the manufacturing belt appear to be downward transitional areas at this time. For example, in recent years the Newark, Buffalo, Providence, Cleveland, and Detroit metropolitan areas have all experienced a serious erosion of economic activity along with high unemployment rates and an out-migration of people and industry. These cities are all characterized by aging industrial facilities, environmental and physical degradation, and some degree of social conflict.

Special problem areas are in some sense anomalous to the system as a whole. They often include regions along national borders and regions isolated from the mainstream of the national economic system. The U.S. border with Mexico is perhaps the major special problem region in the country today. Several decades ago, the Tennessee Valley, the Ozarks, and the Appalachian regions were considered special problem areas and received large amounts of federal aid. But these areas now appear to be in an upward transitional phase as a result of their increasing integration with the national economy.

CONCLUSION

This chapter has attempted to put contemporary migration and regional adjustment into a historical and theoretical perspective.

Migration has been common throughout U.S. history. These flows have always had differential impacts on the regions people were leaving and the regions to which they were going. The major difference today is that since overall population growth has slowed to a trickle, one region's gain is another's loss.

Several theories of regional economic development have been reviewed to see if they shed any light on the problems of regional adjustment in the United States today: stages-of-growth, income inequality, export base, and Schumpeter's creative destruction. No one of these growth theories offers a complete explanation of regional growth and decline in the United States, but together they seem to indicate that market and institutional forces have a much stronger impact on the redistribution of people and economic activity than does federal spending or public policy generally.

NOTES

1. U.S. Department of Commerce, Bureau of the Census, *Historical Statistics of the United States* (Washington, D.C.: US. G.P.O., 1975), A 29–42, 10.
2. Census, *Historical Statistics*, C 1–14, 89.
3. Census, *Historical Statistics*, A 57–72, 11.
4. David Ward, *Cities and Immigrants* (New York: Oxford University Press, 1971), 52.

5. Census, *Historical Statistics,* C 1–14, 89.

6. Ward, *Cities and Immigrants,* 58.

7. Christopher Clayton, "The Structure of Interstate and Interregional Migration: 1965–1970," *Annals of Regional Science* (March 1977): 110.

8. U.S. Department of Commerce, Bureau of the Census, *Current Population Reports,* Ser. P25, No. 640, 1976, and No. 944, 1984.

9. Simon Kuznets, "Introduction: Population Redistribution, Migration, and Economic Growth," in Hope Eldridge and Dorothy S. Thomas, *Demographic Analysis and Interrelations,* Vol. III of *Population Redistribution and Economic Growth: Unitd States, 1870–1950,* (Philadelphia: American Philosophical Society, 1964), xxx.

10. See Chapter 1, Table 1.7.

11. The taxonomy used in the following discussion is adapted in part from D.E. Keeble, "Models of Economic Development," in Richard J. Chorley and Peter Haggett, eds., *Socio-Economic Models in Geography* (London: Methuen, 1967), 77–91.

12. W.W. Rostow, *The Stages of Economic Growth* (Cambridge: Cambridge University Press, 1960).

13. Rowstow, *Stages,* 7.

14. Rostow, *Stages,* 39.

15. Kirkpatrick Sale, *Power Shift* (New York: Random House, 1975), 25.

16. For further discussion of the business climate, see Chapter 4.

17. Rostow, *Stages,* 9.

18. William H. Miernyk, *The Changing Structure of the Southern Economy* (Research Triangle Park, N.C.: Southern Growth Policies Board, 1977), 8.

19. For a summary of these criticisms, see D.E. Keeble, "Models of Economic Development," 251–53.

20. See Douglas C. North, "Location Theory and Regional Growth," *Journal of Political Economy* 63, 3 (June 1955): 243–258; and Harvey Perloff and Lowdon Wingo, Jr., "Natural Resource Endowment and Regional Economic Growth," in Joseph J. Spengler, ed., *Natural Resources and Economic Growth,* (Washington, D.C.: Resources for the Future, 1961), 191–212.

21. Perloff and Wingo, "Natural Resource Endowment," 200–201.

22. See Lorna Monti, "How Oil Supports Prosperity in Texas," *Texas Business Review* LI, 1 (January 1977): 14–22.

23. Perloff and Wingo, "Natural Resource Endowment," 206.

24. Jean Fourastie, *Le Grand Espoir de XXᵉ Siecle* (Paris, 1950), 92–93.

25. Miernyk, *Changing Structure,* 6–7.

26. For instance, E.F. Heckscher, "The Effect of Foreign Trade on the Distribution of Income," *Ekonomisk Tidskrift* XXI (1919): 497–512; B. Ohlin, *Interregional and International Trade* (Cambridge, Mass.: Harvard University Press, 1933); B. Balassa, *The Theory of Economic Integration* (Homewood, Ill.: R.D. Irwin, 1961).

27. E. Evan Brunson and Thomas D. Bever, *Southern Growth Trends: 1970–76* (Research Triangle Park, N.C.: Southern Growth Policies Board, 1978).

28. See Gunnar Myrdal, *Economic Theory and Underdeveloped Regions* (London: Duckworth, 1957), and Albert O. Hirschman, *The Strategy of Economic Development* (New Haven, Conn.: Yale University Press, 1958).

29. Myrdal, *Economic Theory,* 34.

30. Hirschman, *Strategy,* 183–84.

31. Hirschman, *Strategy,* 184–88.

32. August Losch, *The Economics of Location,* trans. William H. Woglom (New Haven, Conn.: Yale University Press, 1956).

33. Schumpeter's major works relating to the problem of economic development are *The The-*

ory of Economic Development (Cambridge, Mass.: Harvard University Press, 1934), *Business Cycles* (New York: McGraw-Hill, 1939), and *Capitalism, Socialism, and Democracy* (New York: Harper and Brothers, 1947).

34. Schumpeter, *Capitalism, Socialism, and Democracy*, 132.

35. See Mancur Olson, *The Causes and Quality of Southern Growth* (Research Triangle Park, N.C.: Southern Growth Policies Board, 1977).

36. See, for example, Lester Thurow, *The Zero-Sum Society: Distribution and the Possibilities for Economic Change* (New York: Basic Books, 1980); Robert Reich, *The Next American Frontier* (New York: Times Books, 1983); and Barry Bluestone and Bennett Harrison, *The Deindustrialization of America: Plant Closings, Community Abandonment, and the Dismantling of Basic Industries* (New York: Basic Books, 1982).

37. For instance, Bluestone and Harrison, *The Deindustrialization of America*.

38. Thurow and Reich, for example, advocate the revitalization of the Depression-era Reconstruction Finance Corporation to allocate funds among "sunset" and "sunrise" industries.

39. See Joseph A. Schumpeter, *Business Cycles;* Raymond Vernon, "International Investment and International Trade in the Product Cycle," *Quarterly Journal of Economics* 46 (May 1966): 113–119; Seev Hirsch, *Location of Industry and International Competitiveness* (Oxford: Clarendon Press, 1967); and John Rees, "Decision Making, the Growth of the Firm and the Business Environment," in F.E.I. Hamilton, ed., *Spatial Perspectives on Industrial Organization and Decision Making* (London: Wiley, 1974).

40. See John Rees and Howard A. Stafford, *A Review of Regional Growth and Industrial Location Theory: Towards Understanding the Development of High-Technology Complexes in the United States* (Washington, D.C.: U.S. Congress, Office of Technology Assessment, 1983); John Rees, "Regional Industrial Shifts in the U.S. and the Internal Generation of Manufacturing in Growth Centers of the Southwest," in W. Wheaton, ed., *Interregional Movements and Regional Growth* (Washington, D.C.: Urban Institute, 1979).

41. Rees, "Regional Industrial Shifts," 51–73.

42. See John Friedmann, *Urbanization, Planning, and National Development* (Beverly Hills, Calif.: Sage, 1973), and *Regional Development Policy: A Case Study of Venezuela* (Cambridge, Mass.: MIT Press, 1966).

43. Friedmann, *Regional Development Policy*, 39–44.

3

Technological Change
and Regional Development
in the United States

INTRODUCTION

It was not until Joseph Schumpeter's seminal work on the process of creative destruction that technology was recognized as an important factor of production resulting in economic growth.[1] Indeed, the study of technological change and its impact remained among the terrae incognitae of modern economics and geography until quite recently. Robert Solow found that nearly 85 percent of U.S. economic growth between 1909 and 1949 was a function of technical change, while Nathan Rosenberg noted that "the productivity-increasing impact of technological change has had major effects on the structure and organization of our modern economic system."[2] It is the contention of this chapter that in the same way technological change results in productivity increases and real economic growth at the national level, regional differences in the propensity to create and use new technologies can result in major differences in regional economic growth rates. To date, however, there has been a lack of empirical evidence linking changes in technology to a region's economic health.

Over the last several years the pangs of decline in the nation's industrial heartland as well as increasing growth rates in other parts of the country have given rise to a number of "new" strategies designed to enhance the economic performance of states and localities. Some of these new economic development strategies have focused on a region's capacity to attract high technology industries, though many of these appear as either new wine in old bottles or old wine in new bottles. High technology industries (or, more appropriately, new technology industries) have been posited as a panacea for both the salvation of older industrial areas and the continued growth of the newer areas of the South and West. Some have argued that more policies of the federal government should be aimed at encouraging the growth of high technology companies, while other policy makers and scientists have become more concerned about the social and economic impacts that technological change can bring to different localities. The high anxiety over high technology continues into the 1980s; there is much we still do not understand about the development of high technology complexes, the spread of innovations, the impact of technological change on labor creation, and the role of public policy in stimulating innovation and economic growth. The goal of this chapter is to shed more light on these relatively undefined relationships.

CONCEPTUAL AND OPERATIONAL ISSUES PERTAINING TO HIGH TECHNOLOGY

In studying the link between technological change and regional development, one quickly becomes cognizant of the many conceptual and operational difficulties in defining the relationships among innovation, diffusion, and economic growth. Some of the more constructive work on the relationships between technological change and economic growth has been undertaken by economists at the sector and company level.[3] The focus of many of these studies has been the creation of new technology through the process of invention, patenting, and imitation. Research and development funding (hereafter referred to as R & D) has been examined primarily in terms of aggregate interindustry and interfirm differences. In addition, problems of measuring innovation output and productivity have been analyzed, and the relationship between firm size and innovation has been examined.[4] The last topic, the relationship between market structure and innovation, has resulted in a number of different findings, including definitive relationships between R & D expenditures and firm/industry growth rates. R & D spending tends to be higher within growth industries where technological change tends to be rapid. Larger firms, however, have not always led their industries in their propensity to innovate.[5] Therefore, independent entrepreneurs and small firms are prominent contributors to the development of new technology.[6]

One of the major problems with research on technological change is the incrementalism or continuity problem implicit in the definition of innovation, that is, the way an innovation itself can change during the process of diffusion and adoption. A related problem is that an imitation rather than innovation strategy may be quicker, cheaper, and less risky for potential innovators. Levitt reminds us that "by far the greatest flow of newness is not innovation at all. Rather it is imitation. . . . IBM got into computers as an imitator; Texas Instruments into transitors as an imitator. We often mistake innovation for what is really imitation."[7] Levitt's work and that of others suggest that imitation is epidemic, and can be viewed as "reverse R & D," where firms work back from what others have done and in many cases come up with better products. The real difference between an innovation and an imitation strategy, then, is one of the more difficult operational issues that surround research on technological change and its impacts.

Most of the work by economists has inevitably been nonspatial in nature. More recently geographers and regional scientists have become increasingly concerned with the conceptual and empirical issues relating technological change and regional development. The roots of such work can be traced to the early work of growth pole theorists and the premise that the propulsive nature of key growth sectors would have a major impact on both the generation and the spread or diffusion of innovations.[8] More empirically based research in Britain has suggested that many of the factors influencing the innovation adoption process vary among regions in a systematic manner.[9] Such factors include the location of company headquarters and R & D facilities relative to branch plants. There is also evidence that interregional contrasts in manufacturing productivity may be related to the failure of plants in some areas to adopt the latest production techniques. Because the propensity to innovate varies among industries, it follows that the industrial structure of a region can have a major impact on innovation generation and diffusion. One of the reasons why a paucity of empirical research exists on the link between technology and regional change in the United States lies in the plethora of ways that new or high technology can be defined.

ON DEFINING NEW AND HIGH TECHNOLOGY

Most discussions of this topic start with the premise that there is no single, generally accepted definition of "high technology." One definition of high technology used by Congress's Office of Technology Assessment includes "companies that are engaged in the design, development and introduction of new products and/or innovative manufacturing processes through the systematic application of scientific and technical knowledge. . . ."[10] Such companies use state-of-the-art techniques, have a high proportion of R&D costs, employ a high proportion of scientific, technical, and engineering personnel, and serve small, specialized markets. Nevertheless, the popular image of the term "high technology" refers mostly to high *product* technology and not high *process* technology industries, a category that also needs to be included because of the use of advanced production methods.

Most studies agree, however, that a number of variables should influence the definition of new or high technology industries. Two variables in particular stand out: the use of R&D spending relative to company sales and the number of technical workers as a proportion of total employment. This latter indicator usually implies the proportion of scientists, engineers, and other technical personnel in the work force.[11] While information on labor content is important in defining high technology industries, any definition that relies solely on the human capital component should be open to question.

A recent study by the Bureau of Labor Statistics comes up with a comprehensive definition of high technology industries made up of forty-seven sectors at the 3-digit level of the Standard Industrial Classification (SIC) and one four-digit sector.[12] Most of the industries listed (Table 3.1) also appear in other classifications. This typology was based on the use of three criteria:

1. R&D expenditures, where the ratio of R&D expenditures to net sales was at least twice the average for all industries;
2. the use of scientific and technical personnel, where the number of technology-oriented workers accounted for a proportion of total employment that was at least one and a half times the average for all industries; and
3. the degree of product sophistication relative to the utilization of technology-oriented workers and R&D expenditures.

The BLS study produced a list of three-digit SIC sectors because appropriate data were not available at the four-digit level. However, studies using variations on this methodology tend to come up with a definition of high technology industry that includes four-digit sectors that are part of the sectors identified in Table 3.1. The BLS study also goes one step further than most studies in recognizing the propulsive nature of certain industries within the service sector. The production of computer software, for example, is a highly innovative, high-growth industry. Yet this highly propulsive industry remains hidden in SIC 737 and tends to be excluded from studies of high technology that focus only on the manufacturing sector. Indeed, studies that focus on high technology industries generally tend to underestimate the innovative potential of other business or producer service industries.

Table 3.1 does not suffer as much as other typologies. These problems have been touched upon before, and they can be summarized as:

1. the exclusion of key business service sectors like software development;
2. the exclusion of production processes; and
3. the assumption that all high-technology industries are growth industries.

On this last point, many high technology products, particularly in small companies, involve high front-end costs for research, development, and marketing. This implies a high degree of risk that will cause high mortality rates among new technology-based firms such as exists among small businesses in general. When cities and localities search for high technology firms, most are interested in the high growth potential more than the high technology potential. In this regard it is dangerous to equate high technology with high growth, particularly in an employment context when the conventional definition of technological change has been the substitution of capital for labor. According to the BLS study referred

TABLE 3.1
Definitions of High Technology Industries

SIC	Industry	High tech group[a]		
		I	II	III
131	Crude petroleum and natural gas	X		
162	Heavy construction, except highway and street	X		
281	Industrial inorganic chemicals	X		X
282	Plastic materials and synthetics	X		X
283	Drugs	X	X	X
284	Soaps, cleaners, and toilet preparations	X		X
285	Paints and allied products	X		X
286	Industrial organic chemicals	X		X
287	Agricultural chemicals	X		X
289	Miscellaneous chemical products	X		X
291	Petroleum refining	X		X
301	Tires and inner tubes	X		
324	Cement, hydraulic	X		
348	Ordnance and accessories	X		X
351	Engines and turbines	X		X
352	Farm and garden machinery	X		
353	Construction, mining, and material-handing machinery	X		
354	Metalworking machinery	X		
355	Special industry machinery, except metalworking	X		X
356	General industrial machinery	X		
357	Office, computing, and accounting machines	X	X	X
358	Refrigeration and service industry machinery	X		
361	Electric transmission and distribution equipment	X		X
362	Electrical industrial apparatus	X		X
363	Household appliances	X		
364	Electric lighting and wiring equipment	X		
365	Radio and TV receiving equipment	X		X
366	Communication equipment	X	X	X
367	Electronic components and accessories	X	X	X
369	Miscellaneous electrical machinery	X		X

TABLE 3.1 (continued)

SIC	Industry	High tech group[a] I	II	III
371	Motor vehicles and equipment	X		
372	Aircraft and parts	X	X	X
376	Guided missiles and space vehicles	X	X	X
381	Engineering, laboratory, scientific and research instruments	X		X
382	Measuring and controlling instruments	X		X
383	Optical instruments and lenses	X		X
384	Surgical, medical, and dental instruments	X		X
386	Photographic equipment and supplies	X		X
483	Radio and TV broadcasting	X		
489	Communication services, not elsewhere classified	X		
491	Electric services	X		
493	Combination electric, gas, and other utility services	X		
506	Wholesale trade, electrical goods	X		
508	Wholesale trade machinery, equipment, and supplies	X		
737	Computer and data processing services	X		X
7391	Research and development laboratories	X		X
891	Engineering, architectural, and surveying services	X		
892	Noncommercial educational, scientific, and research organizations	X		

[a]Group 1 includes industries with a proportion of technology-oriented workers (engineers, life and physical scientists, mathematical scientists, engineering and science technicians, and computer specialists) at least 1.5 times the average for all industries. Group II includes industries with a ratio of R&D expenditures to net sales at least twice the average for all industries. Group III includes manufacturing industries with a proportion of technology-oriented workers equal to or greater than the average for all manufacturing industries, and a ratio of R&D expenditures to sales close to or above the average for all industries. Two nonmanufacturing industries that provide technical support to high tech manufacturing industries are also included.

Source: Monthly Labor Review (Nov. 1983).

to earlier, high technology industries are expected to provide only a small proportion of the jobs created between 1982 and 1995.

The impact of high technology industries on employment is discussed later in this chapter. First we turn to the question of the geographical incidence of high technology industries.

THE GEOGRAPHY OF HIGH TECHNOLOGY INDUSTRIES

Until the recent upsurge of interest in attracting high technology industries into particular states and localities, little was known about the geographical patterns of high technology development. Indeed, until the recent release of two studies by researchers at the Brookings Institution and the University of California at Berkeley, we knew more about the spatial incidence of R&D than about high technology industries themselves.

The Geography of Research and Development in the United States

Clearly, understanding the R&D process is a major step toward understanding the generation of new technology. Since federal R&D spending has accounted for over 50 percent of total spending on R&D in the United States in the past twenty-five years, it is not surprising that governmental funding of R&D, like other types of federal spending, has a strong impact on urban and regional development processes. The National Science Foundation has monitored changes in R&D spending in the post-World War II period on an annual basis, but its analysis of geographic distributions has been sketchy at best and limited to the state level. Differences in R&D spending at the metropolitan scale in the United States have only been monitored recently, and this attempt has largely been restricted to the work of Edward Malecki.[13]

The geographical distribution of total federal R&D spending by state for 1970 and 1980 is shown in Table 3.2, based on the annual surveys of science resources carried out by the National Science Foundation.

Predictably, perhaps, in 1980 California received the most R&D support, $7.1 billion out of a total national budget of $30.5 billion (a 23 percent share). A further eight states—Maryland, Massachusetts, New York, Florida, Texas, Pennsylvania, Ohio, and Virginia—each showed more than $1 billion in federal obligations. The twenty leading states together received 87 percent of total federal R&D funds in 1980, and roughly the same pattern persisted throughout the 1970–80 period. California's share of the total R&D budget has indeed fluctuated over time, from 35 percent in 1963 to 21 percent in 1972, to 23 percent in 1980. Maryland's increased share of federal R&D funds can be directly attributed to the overspill of federal R&D installations from Washington, D.C., mostly intramural installations. These include the National Institute of Health, the Naval Air Test Center, the Army Arsenal Labs, the National Bureau of Standards, and

TABLE 3.2
Federal R&D Obligations by Region and State, Selected Years, 1970–80
(In Million U.S. Dollars)

Region and State	1970	1979	Average Annual Percent Change 1970–79	1980
Northeast				
New England:	1,000.8	2,685.1	11.6	2,814.4
Connecticut	160.0	328.4	8.3	470.3
Maine	13.3	23.1	6.4	25.9
Massachusetts	760.9	2,062.3	11.7	2,066.7
New Hampshire	27.3	94.1	14.8	50.2
Rhode Island	29.9	140.7	18.8	149.9
Vermont	9.5	36.5	16.2	51.3
Middle Atlantic:	2,516.0	3,112.3	2.4	3,260.0
New Jersey	741.7	649.3	−1.5	729.4
New York	1,235.6	1,363.1	1.1	1,471.2
Pennsylvania	538.8	1,099.9	8.3	1,059.4
North Central				
East North Central:	1,038.8	2,097.8	8.1	2,316.2
Illinois	239.6	547.2	9.6	599.9
Indiana	91.6	122.0	3.2	162.4
Michigan	162.8	264.4	5.5	377.5
Ohio	457.3	1,053.2	9.7	1,054.7
Wisconsin	87.1	111.0	2.7	121.7
West North Central:	475.4	1,277.8	11.6	1,618.5
Iowa	32.7	84.9	11.2	121.7
Kansas	16.6	136.3	26.3	353.6
Minnesota	109.3	202.8	7.1	261.6
Missouri	291.2	778.9	11.6	801.6
Nebraska	10.6	31.3	12.7	31.6
North Dakota	8.9	33.4	15.9	38.7
South Dakota	6.1	10.2	5.9	9.9
South				
South Atlantic:	2,899.3	5,726.9	7.9	6,430.2
Delaware	16.3	14.4	−1.4	20.8
District of Columbia	468.5	768.4	5.7	807.0
Florida	824.8	1,017.3	2.4	1,323.5
Georgia	72.3	184.4	11.0	169.8
Maryland	1,063.4	2,359.8	9.3	2,595.0
North Carolina	63.9	220.9	14.8	227.7

TABLE 3.2 (continued)

Region and State	1970	1979	Average Annual Percent Change 1970–79	1980
South Carolina	17.8	114.3	22.9	87.5
Virginia	352.7	940.3	11.5	1,047.1
West Virginia	19.6	107.2	20.7	152.0
East South Central:	599.7	1,347.3	9.4	1,492.8
Alabama	357.2	559.6	5.1	552.7
Kentucky	20.4	43.0	8.6	107.9
Mississippi	28.3	100.7	15.2	109.3
Tennessee	193.8	644.1	14.3	722.9
West South Central:	834.9	1,454.2	6.4	1,585.4
Arkansas	9.8	37.3	16.0	30.0
Louisiana	146.5	209.1	4.0	269.8
Oklahoma	29.5	70.1	10.1	94.5
Texas	649.1	1,137.7	6.4	1,191.3
West				
Mountain:	1,136.7	2,262.7	7.9	2,568.2
Arizona	72.8	201.4	12.0	334.6
Colorado	274.1	442.2	5.5	573.7
Idaho	75.0	147.1	7.8	147.7
Montana	11.6	41.6	15.2	45.7
Nevada	190.9	222.1	1.7	214.5
New Mexico	445.0	955.5	8.9	954.2
Utah	61.1	211.6	14.8	243.9
Wyoming	7.2	41.0	21.4	53.9
Pacific:	4,404.1	7,855.6	6.6	8,272.8
Alaska	43.2	45.9	0.7	42.5
California	3,871.1	6,804.0	6.5	7,138.0
Hawaii	43.8	40.8	−0.8	42.6
Oregon	33.8	100.1	12.8	97.9
Washington	412.2	864.8	8.6	951.8
Outlying areas	17.3	39.4	9.6	45.3
Offices abroad	56.8	57.7	0.2	73.5
U.S. Total	14,980.8	27,916.8	7.2	30,477.3

Source: National Science Foundation. *Research and Development by Industry.* Washington, D.C.: Science Resources Series, 1982.

the National Aeronautics and Space Administration Goddard Space Flight Center. New York State, on the other hand, as might be expected from other indicators of regional economic change, has shown a decline in its share of the total federal R&D pie since the early 1960s. Most of New York's share, however, flows directly into the private sector. "Federal agencies seeking specific kinds of research or development competence to implement their missions have turned to existing organizations with specialized characteristics within certain states. These states contain aircraft, aerospace and electronics industries, concentrations of university research talent, including modern medical research teams and/or geographic areas safe for testing missiles, aircraft, spacecraft and explosives."[14]

Federal R&D allocations are ranked by state for fiscal year 1980 in Table 3.3, along with the rankings of these states in terms of population and total personal income. The data indicate that most of the top recipient R&D states in 1980 also had the larger share of population and income. A major exception is New Mexico, which ranked tenth in federal R&D obligations in 1980, largely due to the presence of Los Alamos National Laboratory, yet the state ranked very low in terms of population and personal income.

Malecki's work on R&D activities at the metropolitan scale brings out even more evidence of geographical concentration.[15] In the United States, as in other countries, R&D was found to be much more concentrated geographically than either population or industrial activity. This results in a form of breeder reaction in which the agglomeration of R&D personnel fosters further local spinoffs of innovation activity, which in turn attract more research-oriented companies and funding to an area.

Of the nearly 6,000 industrial R&D labs in the United States in 1975, Malecki found 88 percent to be located in 177 Standard Metropolitan Statistical Areas (SMSAS); urban areas with more than forty labs were generally found within the manufacturing belt. Urban areas in the South and Southwest, on the other hand, contained only a few concentrations of industrial R&D. The urban locations of the greatest R&D agglomerations among major R&D-performing firms in 1965 and 1977 together with the number of R&D labs are shown in Table 3.4.

In a series of regression analyses, Malecki found that the number of R&D labs per capita and the number of R&D employees relative to total urban population were significantly associated with the proportion of the work force employed in manufacturing and the number of research universities in the various SMSAs as well as the dollar amounts of R&D spent at those universities. These two factors in particular, together with the proximity of R&D labs to corporate headquarters, help explain the continued predominance of the northeastern United States as the area of greatest R&D concentration during the 1960s and 1970s. "That region, despite its recent apparent decline in 'other economic' indicators, appears to be maintaining its traditional importance in industrial R & D. Outside the Northeast, the characteristics favorable to industrial R & D are found

TABLE 3.3
Federal R&D Obligations Compared with Other National Indicators by State, Fiscal Year 1980

State	Total Federal R&D Obligations		Population		Total Personal Income[a]	
	Rank	Percent of Total	Rank	Percent of Total	Rank	Percent of Total
U.S. Total	$30,477 million		[b]227 million		$2,162,936 million	
California	1	23.42	1	10.45	1	12.00
Maryland	2	8.51	18	1.86	16	2.04
Massachusetts	3	6.78	11	2.53	10	2.69
New York	4	4.83	2	7.75	2	8.35
Florida	5	4.34	7	4.34	8	4.10
Texas	6	3.91	3	6.28	3	6.29
Pennsylvania	7	3.48	4	5.24	5	5.19
Ohio	8	3.46	6	4.76	6	4.73
Virginia	9	3.44	14	2.36	11	2.33
New Mexico	10	3.13	37	0.57	37	0.47
Washington	11	3.12	20	1.82	18	1.97
District of Columbia	12	2.65	47	0.28	43	0.36
Missouri	13	2.63	15	2.17	14	2.05
New Jersey	14	2.39	9	3.25	9	3.73
Tennessee	15	2.37	17	2.03	22	1.64
Illinois	16	1.97	5	5.04	4	5.57
Colorado	17	1.88	28	1.27	24	1.34
Alabama	18	1.81	22	1.72	23	1.35
Connecticut	19	1.54	25	1.37	20	1.69
Michigan	20	1.24	8	4.09	7	4.27
Kansas	21	1.16	32	1.04	30	1.09
Arizona	22	1.10	29	1.20	29	1.11
Louisiana	23	0.89	19	1.86	21	1.65
Minnesota	24	0.86	21	1.80	19	1.84
Utah	25	0.80	36	0.64	36	0.52
North Carolina	26	0.75	10	2.59	13	2.13
Nevada	27	0.70	43	0.35	41	0.40

TABLE 3.3 (continued)

State	Total Federal R&D Obligations		Population		Total Personal Income[a]	
	Rank	Percent of Total	Rank	Percent of Total	Rank	Percent of Total
Georgia	28	0.56	13	2.41	15	2.04
Indiana	29	0.53	12	2.42	12	2.27
West Virginia	30	NA		NA		NA
Rhode Island	31	0.49	40	0.42	39	0.41
Idaho	32	0.48	41	0.42	44	0.35
Iowa	33	0.40	27	1.29	27	1.26
Wisconsin	34	0.40	16	2.08	17	2.04
Mississippi	35	0.36	31	1.11	33	0.77
Kentucky	36	0.35	23	1.62	25	1.29
Oregon	37	0.32	30	1.16	28	1.14
Oklahoma	38	0.31	26	1.34	26	1.28
South Carolina	39	0.29	24	1.38	31	1.05
Wyoming	40	0.18	50	0.21	49	0.24
Vermont	41	0.17	49	0.23	51	0.19
New Hampshire	42	0.16	42	0.41	42	0.39
Montana	43	0.15	44	0.35	45	0.31
Hawaii	44	0.14	39	0.43	38	0.45
Alaska	45	0.14	51	0.18	50	0.24
North Dakota	46	0.13	46	0.29	47	0.26
Nebraska	47	0.10	35	0.69	35	0.68
Arkansas	48	0.10	33	1.01	32	0.77
Maine	49	0.09	38	0.50	40	0.41
Delaware	50	0.07	48	0.26	46	0.29
South Dakota	51	0.03	45	0.31	48	0.25
Outlying areas and offices abroad	—	0.39	—	—	—	—

[a]Data shown as of December 31, 1980. See U.S. Department of Commerce, Bureau of Economic Analysis, *U.S. Department of Commerce News*, August 9, 1981 (BEA 81–45).

[b]Provisional estimate of resident population as of July 1, 1980. See U.S. Department of Commerce, Bureau of the Census, *Current Population Reports*, Ser. P-25.

Sources: U.S. Department of Commerce, U.S. Department of the Treasury, and National Science Foundation.

TABLE 3.4
Locations of Greatest R&D Agglomeration Among Major R&D-Performing Firms, 1965 and 1977

	1965			1977	
Rank	SMSA	Number of Laboratories	Rank	SMSA	Number of Laboratories
1.	New York-Newark-Jersey City	161	1.	New York-Newark-Jersey City	147
2.	Los Angeles-Long Beach-Anaheim	78	2.	Los Angeles-Long Beach-Anaheim	108
3.	Chicago-Gary	67	3.	Chicago-Gary	81
4.	Philadelphia-Wilmington-Trenton	62	4.	Philadelphia-Wilmington-Trenton	72
5.	Boston-Lawrence-Lowell	51	5.	San Francisco-Oakland-San Jose	64
6.	San Francisco-Oakland-San Jose	45	6.	Boston-Lawrence-Lowell	58
7.	Detroit-Ann Arbor	40	7.	Cleveland-Akron-Lorain	53
8.	Cleveland-Akron-Lorain	33	8.	Detroit-Ann Arbor	52
9.	Pittsburgh	30	9.	Pittsburgh	31
10.	Houston-Galveston	21	10.	Houston-Galveston	30
11.	Baltimore	20	11.	Milwaukee-Racine	23
12.	Hartford-Springfield	18	11.	Hartford-Springfield	23
13.	Albany-Schenectady-Troy	16	13.	St. Louis	22
13.	Washington	16	13.	Washington	22
13.	Minneapolis-St. Paul	16	15.	Minneapolis-St. Paul	19
16.	Buffalo	14	16.	Dayton	18
17.	St. Louis	12	17.	Cincinnati-Hamilton	17
18.	Milwaukee-Racine	11	17.	San Diego	17
19.	Dayton	10	17.	Bridgeport-New Haven	17
19.	Denver-Boulder	10	20.	Albany-Schenectady-Troy	16
19.	Indianapolis	10			

Source: Edward J. Malecki, "Recent Trends in the Location of Industrial Research and Development: Regional Development Implications for the United States," in J. Rees, G.J.D. Hewings, and H.A. Stafford. *Industrial Location and Regional Systems* (New York: J.F. Bergin, 1981) p. 226.

in relatively few urban areas.''[16] In a related study, evidence is shown that industrial R&D is evolving away from its dependence on some large city regions, especially New York, though R&D still remains basically a large-city activity.[17] This apparent decentralization of R&D away from large urban areas like New York, Boston, and Los Angeles to other large cities in the Midwest and the Sunbelt suggests that a critical threshold of indigenous technological capacity required by high technology industries may now be available in a greater number of urban areas across the United States. A recent report by the Federal Reserve Bank of Boston suggest, however, that increased employment in high tech industries in the Great Lakes states at least will only be a small part of the answer to that region's economic problems.[18]

Geographical Variations in High Technology Industries

It is only very recently that comprehensive analyses of the geography of high technology industries in the United States have been conducted. Using a large data set on individual plants and companies, Catherine Armington and her colleagues at the Brookings Institution have examined regional differences in the formation and growth of high technology businesses.[19] Adopting a broad definition of high technology industries comparable to that included in Table 3.1 (based on technical employment and R&D expenditures per four-digit SIC sector), they have found that the distribution of high technology jobs across the four major census regions of the United States corresponds closely to that of employment in all industries, that is, high technology industry was found to be dispersed across the country in rough proportion to the distribution of all industries. This is very different from the pattern for R&D, which does not include the dispersed pattern of branch plants implicit in high technology industrial production.

Table 3.5 summarizes the employment growth trends by region over 1976–

TABLE 3.5
Employment Growth Shares by Region, 1976–80

Region	High Technology		All Industries	
	Share of Employment	Share of Growth	Share of Employment	Share of Growth
U.S. total	100%	100%	100%	100%
Northeast	29	11	25	10
North Central	28	18	28	22
South	24	42	31	38
West	19	29	17	30

Source: Catherine Armington, C. Harris, and M. Odle, *Formation and Growth in High Technology Industries: A Regional Assessment* (Washington, D.C.: Brookings Institution, 1983).

80 for both the high technology sectors and total industrial activity. The Northeast has 29 percent, North Central 28 percent, South 24 percent, and the West 19 percent of high technology industry. Since the Brookings study could relate branch plants to their headquarters, they also found that high technology plants in the South census region were owned by out-of-state companies to a far higher degree than such plants in other regions. This tends to confirm the high incidence of branch plants in the South, as suggested by other work, and hence the *de jure* external control of employment levels in these plants by decision makers in distant locations.[20] Table 3.5 also shows that the two regions with the lowest shares of high technology industry in 1976 experienced the largest growth rate during 1976–1980, disclosing a tendency toward regional convergence. Although the South had only a 24 percent share of high technology employment, its share of growth in these sectors was 42 percent.

The Brookings study also shows that although the Northeast region used to have a large enough share of high-growth industries to offset its higher share of low-growth manufacturing, the region's advantage in industrial mix had decreased further by 1980, confirming a trend discussed earlier by Rees.[21] Despite its general economic health, the South continued to show only a small share of the high-growth industries, in contrast to the West, which displayed a much more favorable industrial mix. The rates of formation of new high technology firms were also found to be inversely related to regional shares of high technology in 1976. The Northeast and North Central had formation rates below the national average, while the South and West had above-average rates of business establishments and job creation.

The Brookings study also included a more disaggregated analysis of high technology development at the metropolitan scale for a sample of thirty-five SMSAs. Business formations and job creations were related to a number of contextual variables that included the pool of potential entrepreneurs, the costs of doing business (wage rates, utility costs, and local taxes), industrial activity levels, the labor force, and the general attractiveness of a city as well as other regional economic conditions. In their regression analyses, the relative attractiveness of the city both to people and to business (as measured by the rate of population growth in the first half of the 1970s) was the factor most strongly related to urban differences in business formation rates. Though it is generally assumed that a large agglomeration effect exists in the formation of high technology business, the Brookings study found no measurable association of high technology business formations with the local employment share in high tech industries. Indeed, negative relationships were found between growth rates and sector shares; that is, in areas where the high technology sector had a relatively large share of total local employment, its growth rate was generally lower than average. As might be expected, however, employment growth in large high technology firms was seen to be highly responsive to variations in the strength of the local economy and in the supply of technically skilled labor.

Another study undertaken to examine differences in the location of high technology industries also highlights the diverse nature of the high technology sector.[22] This study (referred to hereafter as the Berkeley study) used a different data souce than the Brookings study, specifically the 1972 and 1977 Census of Manufactures. The data set does not allow one to address headquarters–branch plant relationships, nor does it include some critical business service sectors discussed earlier. But the Census of Manufacturers is generally regarded as the most accurate secondary data set on manufacturing industry.

The Berkeley study uses an entropy index to measure the spatial dispersion of high technology industries for 100 four-digit sectors across all 3,140 counties of the United States between 1972 and 1977. Individual high tech industries show a large degree of dispersion across the United States, with missiles and space vehicle parts being the most concentrated industry in 1977 and fertilizers the most dispersed. "In the middle range lie many of those high-tech industries which are most innovative and fastest growing. Computers, semi-conductors, biological products, measuring devices, industrial controls, optical instruments and machine tools are all only moderately dispersed compared to the average for all high-tech industries."[23]

In analyzing the distribution of high tech industries at the metropolitan scale, the Berkeley study identifies a set of winners and losers of high tech jobs and plants between 1972 and 1977 using a threefold division of urban areas: big city SMSAs, adjacent or suburban SMSAs, and independent noncontiguous SMSAs. The middle category of adjacent/suburban SMSAs and the newer big-city SMSAs were more prominent generators of absolute job gain. The top ten net employment winners and losers of high tech industry between 1972 and 1977, shown in Table 3.6, include such inevitable SMSAs as San Jose, California (largely synonymous with Silicon Valley), and Anaheim, California, together with Worcester, Massachusetts. Many of the most technology-intensive places (with a high proportion of the labor force in high tech activities) are also among the smallest and medium-sized SMSAs, and they are more likely to be found in the Midwest and South than in othe parts of the country. Although most of the top ten metro areas with the highest absolute changes in high tech employment are predictable from popular conceptions (Table 3.6), some, like Oklahoma City and Lakeland, Florida, may not be. Many of the largest losers in Table 3.6 may also be predictable: New York City, Cleveland, Baltimore, and Jersey City. But the big losers are not all frostbelt cities, since Table 3.6 includes Miami, and Los Angeles. Furthermore, many of the totals in the list of losers are so small that they could be unduly influenced by recessionary cutbacks in one or two large plants, a factor that could be identified if the data from the Brookings study could be merged with that from Berkeley. The findings of the Berkeley study also suggests that the popularized high tech war between the states might break down on an east-west rather than a north-south axis across the country.

The Berkeley study also attempts the massive task of explaining the location factors behind the complex, dispersed pattern of high tech jobs around the

TABLE 3.6
Top Ten Net Employment Winners and Losers in High Technology, 1972–77

Winners		Losers	
San Jose, Cal.	31,909	New York, N.Y.	−8,975
Anaheim, Cal.	30,612	Philadelphia, Pa.	−8,586
Houston, Tex.	18,932	Cleveland, Oh.	−8,170
San Diego, Cal.	16,782	Miami, Fla.	−6,584
Boston, Mass.	15,173	Syracuse, N.Y.	−5,521
Dallas, Tex.	12,067	Baltimore, Md.	−4,245
Worcester, Mass.	9,893	Jersey City, N.J.	−4,062
Oklahoma City, Ok.	8,363	Parkersburg, W. Va.-Oh.	−3,664
Lakeland, Fla.	8,132	Los Angeles, Cal.	−3,220
Phoenix, Ariz.	7,976	Decatur, Ill.	−3,130
Median gain	248	Median loss	740

Source: Amy Glasmeier, P. Hall, and A. Markusen, *Recent Evidence on High Technology Industries Spatial Tendencies: A Preliminary Investigation* (Berkeley: University of California, 1983).

country using a large number of variables in a series of regression analyses. The variables include labor supply (wage rates, unionization, and unemployment rates), business climate (as measured by the presence of specialized buisness services, research facilities, and defense spending), infrastructure factors (transportation networks and utility rates), amenity features (cultural amenities, housing prices, pollution levels, mild climates, and good schools), and a number of other socioeconomic variables (including minority populations and conservative voting patterns). Regression analyses based on such a large number of variables (nineteen) are always open to question, but the complexity of the location patterns is confirmed by the fact that only two variables are consistently significantly related to various measures of high tech location patterns: per capita defense spending and percent black population. The labor force factor and unionization rates were also found to be significant in some of the analyses. The study therefore reaches an appropriate conclusion that "these results offer strong support for our view that individual high-tech industries are highly heterogeneous and display quite disparate spatial tendencies *which can only be understood by analyzing disaggregated sectors.*"[24] Hence a major round of research needs to be done to ascertain the real determinants of the various kinds of high tech industries.

The Berkeley study can be criticized for excluding the service sectors and not addressing 1972–77 recessionary job losses that were experienced in over one-third of the industries, but this type of national study, like its Brookings counterpart, is extremely useful in sorting out some of the realities from the myths surrounding the current attention given to the development of high technology industries. We need to know more about specific industries and specific areas of high tech concentration. Despite the fact that the media and other groups keep citing the extraordinary success of Silicon Valley and Route 128, we know very little of the precise historical development of these areas. Recent studies by Nancy Dorfman on Route 128 and by Annalee Saxenian are steps in the right direction,[25] though the Saxenian study is mainly concerned with the dual labor market and other "contradictions" of Silicon Valley. Documentation and mapping of electronics companies in that study rely on articles in the *Los Angeles Times* more than other reputable business directories like Dun and Bradstreet and the Economic Census.

In a background paper for the ongoing study by the Congressional Office of Technology Assessment on Innovation and Regional Economic Development, John Rees and Howard Stafford examine the location factors that influence high technology industries.[26] Locational variables include those related to the friction of distance as well as those related to the attributes of areas: labor availability and cost (considered the most important determining factor in many studies); access to and quality of academic institutions; quality of life and other amenity variables; access to markets, materials, and various transportation networks; taxes and access to development capital. Table 3.7 shows the relative importance of the ten most important factors that influence the location decisions of high tech plants, compiled from two different primary data sources. The sources include an open-ended survey by Howard Stafford of factors influencing decision makers in their choice of high tech and other plant sites as well as a survey by Congress's Joint Economic Committee (JEC) that asked respondents to rank specific location factors. Despite differences in the methodologies of the two studies and regardless of the scale of the location decision, labor stands out in both studies as the most important of the industrial location determinates. No issue is more debated than the influence of local taxation on site selection, but the JEC survey (contrary to most other studies) indicates that taxes are the second most important locational determinant of high technology firms. Stafford's survey, on the other hand, places taxes as a minor locational variable—a difference that may be attributable to differences in the survey design. The JEC study asked an explicit question about taxes, whereas Stafford simply asked respondents to list relevant factors. Stafford contends that taxes are perhaps as much an emotional issue as a financial issue influencing decision makers.[27]

The JEC study also looked at changes in high tech jobs between 1975 and 1979, and at the state level arrived at conclusions similar to the more recent Brookings study. The JEC study defined high tech in a highly aggregated manner, including five two-digit SIC sectors but excluding any service sector.[28] Interstate comparison is included in Table 3.8, the order of the states reflecting their absolute job gains between 1975 and 1979. Although it should be remem-

TABLE 3.7
Factors Influencing Location of New Manufacturing Plants

Rank	Factors	
	High Technology Plants[a]	Non-High Technology Plants[a]
1	Labor	Labor
2	Transportation availability	Market access
3	Quality of life	Transportation availability
4	Markets access	Materials access
5	Utilities	Utilities
6	Site characteristics	Regulatory practice
7	Community characteristics	Quality of life
8	Business climate	Business climate
9	Taxes	Site characteristics
10	Development organizations	Taxes
	High Technology Plants According to the JEC Questionnaire (1982)[b]	
	Selection of Region	Selection Within Region
1	Labor skills/availability	Labor availability
2	Labor costs	State/local tax structure
3	Tax climate within region	Business climate
4	Academic institutions	Cost of property/construction
5	Cost of living	Transport availability for people
6	Transportation	Ample area for expansion
7	Markets access	Proximity to good schools
8	Regional regulatory practices	Proximity to amenities
9	Energy costs/availability	Transport facilities for goods
10	Cultural amenities	Proximity to customers

[a]*Source:* H.A. Stafford, "The Effects of Environmental Regulations on Industrial Location: Survey of 104 Plants." Working Paper (Univ. of Cincinnati, 1983).

[b]*Source:* John Rees and Howard Stafford, *A Review of Regional Growth and Industrial Location Theory: Towards Understanding the Development of High-Technology Complexes in the U.S.* (Washington, D.C.: U.S. Congress Office of Technology Assessment, 1983).

bered that this was generally a time of economic recovery from the great recession of 1975, some striking patterns emerge. California experienced an absolute growth in high tech jobs three times the size of its nearest rival, Massachusetts. The seven leading SMSAs listed in the Berkeley study as high tech winners (Table 3.6) are also located in the top three states in the JEC study. Table 3.8 also shows that though the growth rate in high tech jobs is low in many of the older states of the Northeast and Midwest (New York, New Jersey, Pennsylvania, Ohio,

TABLE 3.8
Changes in High Tech Jobs for Selected States, 1975–79
(In Thousands)

State	1979 Employment	Employment Change 1975–79	Percent Change 1975–79
California	574.9	154.3	36.7
Massachusetts	222.0	54.4	32.5
Texas	143.6	48.0	50.2
Florida	98.3	37.4	61.4
New York	375.0	32.7	9.6
Minnesota	104.8	29.0	38.3
North Carolina	83.7	28.7	52.2
Arizona	57.8	20.5	55.0
Colorado	53.1	20.1	61.0
Michigan	92.3	18.6	25.2
New Hampshire	36.5	16.1	79.0
New Jersey	182.2	15.2	9.1
Connecticut	94.4	14.4	18.0
Pennsylvania	209.9	13.3	6.8
Ohio	161.9	13.0	8.7
Illinois	242.5	12.6	5.5

Source: U.S. Congress, Joint Economic Committee, *Location of High Technology Firms and Regional Economic Development* (Washington, D.C.: U.S. Government Printing Office, 1982).

and Illinois), the absolute number of high tech jobs in these states in 1979 was higher than for any other state bar three (California, Massachusetts, and Texas). The fact that these older industrial states have a large number of high tech jobs already shows that they should by no means be written off as having no potential for further high tech development.

The Spread of New Technology in U.S. Industry

If we have known very little until recently about the incidence of high technology industries in the United States, we know even less about the spread of new technology across various industries and regions of the country. Though economists like Edwin Mansfield and Bela Gold have undertaken numerous studies of the adoption and diffusion of industrial innovations over time, they have ignored the geographical dimension to this diffusion process. Likewise, though geographers have a long tradition of concern for the innovation diffusion process, their research has focused on consumer rather than industrial innovations.[29]

As a step toward understanding more about regional differences in innovation potential in the United States, a recent study of the new computerized production processes in the machinery industries by John Rees, Ronald Briggs, and Raymond Oakey relates the adoption of these innovations to a number of variables: sectoral, organizational, and geographical.[30] A detailed survey of over 600 manufacturing plants in the machinery and electronics industries (SIC 35 and 36) shows some interesting differences in the adoption rates of these new technologies, which include computerized numerical control (CNC) systems; the use of computers in commercial, design, and manufacturing activities; programmable handling systems; and the use of microprocessors in final products. Many of the patterns are intuitively predictable from conventional economic theory; but some are not.

Plants belonging to multiplant firms, with their increased economies of scale and financial fexibility, were much more likely to adopt these new production technologies than plants that represented single-plant firms. For NC (numerical control) machines, the use of computers in design and manufacturing, and programmable handling systems, adoption rates among multiplant firms were double those for single-plant firms. Such a finding was contrary to the popularized notion that small single-plant firms are relatively more innovative than their larger counterparts for all kinds of technologies, and it also points out the importance of distinguishing between product and process innovations, particularly since small firms specialize more in new product technology. Similarly, larger plants had much higher adoption rates than smaller ones, and plants with R&D capability on site or at some other site within the firm had much higher adoption rates than plants with no R&D on site. In fact, 505 plants or 80 percent of the total performed some kind of R&D on site, a proportion higher than expected.

The findings on age of plant (summarized in Table 3.9) showed the least expected and perhaps the most provocative findings to come out of the study. The table illustrates that in plants built in or before 1939, 57 percent had adopted CNC by 1982, whereas in plants built between 1970 and 1981 only 27 percent adopted CNC. The statistical significance refers to a chi square analysis performed on the absolute counts per cell. Nonprogrammable handling systems show no statistically significant differences by age of plant because they include a variety of conventional, mechanical handling systems that tend to be used in most manufacturing plants. On the whole, however, Table 3.9 shows that older plants are more likely to adopt new process technologies than newer ones. Indeed, a progressive inverse relationship exists between the age of a plant and its propensity to adopt new technologies. Such results indicate that for a key part of the durable good sector the older manufacturing plants across the country have been retooling to remain competitive. Much of this retooling can be explained by the fact that most of the new technologies are discrete units that can be introduced into a plant in an incremental fashion without a massive reorganization of total plant layout.

TABLE 3.9
Adoption Rates by Age of Plant

	1939 or Before	1940–49	1950–59	1960–69	1970–81	Significance
NC	59	52	41	33	28	.0001
CNC	57	46	45	37	27	.0001
Computer for Commercial	79	70	67	62	58	.009
Computer for Design	41	30	23	18	14	.0001
Computer for Manufacturing	58	57	45	40	30	.0001
Programmable Handling	9	16	6	5	2	.003
Nonprogrammable Handling	34	49	49	48	46	.150
Microprocessors in Product	31	28	21	28	19	.183
Total Number of Respondents	111	63	109	181	150	

Source: John Rees, Ronald Briggs, and Raymond Oakey, "The Adoption of New Technology in the American Machinery Industry," *Regional Studies* (forthcoming, 1984).

The results clearly imply that older plants in the United States cannot be written off as users of outdated technology and suggest the inherent potential such firms have to increase their technological sophistication. One other explanation for the results shown in Table 3.9 may lie in consolidation or rationalization procedures among multiplant companies. During recessionary periods in particular, this process does go on, but it is doubtful whether such processes could go on with enough magnitude to influence the results shown in Table 3.9.

When adoption rates are compared by region of the country, statistically significant differences only appear for two of the eight technologies studied. Yet there are some important regional differences in the adoption rates for various innovations. Regional differences in the adoption of CNC are indeed statistically significant, with the North Central region showing an adoption rate of 47 percent, the Northeast region 41 percent, the West 37 percent, and the South 28 percent. The high rate for the North Central region is not surprising, given its historic role as the center of the machine tools industry. It is the older industrial regions of the north central and northeastern parts of the manufacturing belt that display the highest propensity to use new production technology, not the growth regions of the South and West. Thus, the innovation capacity of the older industrial heartland should not be overlooked in any attempt at reindustrialization or economic recovery that may be initiated at the federal or state level. These findings also gain support from a study by the Urban Institute on the age structure of regional plant and equipment. "Data on the age of the machine tools provides a different picture of the regional distribution of old capital. . . . The Frostbelt maintained a lead in the percentage of the technologically superior machine tools (CNC). . . .The evidence thus suggests that at least for this one important category of equipment the Frostbelt is at least as modern as the Sunbelt. . . .This strong bias in the distribution of NC tools in favor of the Frostbelt is important in assessing the relative competitiveness of the various regions."[31]

In this diffusion study, Rees and his colleagues examine differences in the adoption rates for the new technologies among regions, controlling for differences in industry size, organizational status, R&D intensity, and age and size of plants.[32] Regional adoption rates by organizational status of plants are shown in Table 3.10, and statistically significant differences between regions are evident among single-plant firms adopting these key technologies: numerical control, CNC, and microprocessors in the final product. It is no coincidence that in the case of NC and CNC, most of the early development work was spawned in the manufacturing belt, whereas for the use of microprocessors in products Massachusetts and California firms appear to have been the most progressive in the development of minicomputers and microcomputers. For smaller, single-plant firms, therefore, the pattern of Table 3.10 suggests a distance decay or local spread effect in adoption patterns; that is, adoption rates are lowest in regions furthest removed from the spawning grounds of these leading edge technologies. The same type of regional differences in adoption rates among the large mul-

TABLE 3.10
Regional Adoption Rates by Organizational Status

	Type of Firm	Northeast	North Central	South	West	Probability
NC	Single-plant firm	27	31	11	17	.02[a]
	Multiplant firm	55	60	49	53	.47
CNC	Single-plant firm	37	37	16	13	.004[a]
	Multiplant firm	47	56	38	60	.06
Computer for Commercial	Single-plant firm	54	58	47	43	.36
	Multiplant firm	70	80	76	80	.52
Computer for Design	Single-plant firm	17	9	10	15	.49
	Multiplant firm	31	36	32	34	.93
Computer for Manufacturing	Single-plant firm	38	32	20	15	.07
	Multiplant firm	57	60	52	55	.76
Programmable Handling	Single-plant firm	3	2	0	3	.37[b]
	Multiplant firm	10	12	7	19	.35
Nonprogrammable Handling	Single-plant firm	37	35	47	47	.30
	Multiplant firm	43	49	61	55	.22
Microprocessors In Product	Single-plant firm	33	16	11	20	.01[a]
	Multiplant firm	29	38	27	27	.33

[a]Statistically significant (using chi square).
[b]More than 20 percent of cells have expected counts less than 5.
Source: Rees, Briggs, and Oakey, "Adoption of New Technology," 1984.

tiplant firms do not show up in Table 3.10, reflecting the ability of these organizations to spread new production technologies throughout a regionally dispersed corporate system. The results of Table 3.10 do suggest, however, that policy makers at the state or federal level who are interested in nurturing small businesses should give some consideration to a technical assistance or technology transfer program that encourages the spread of new technologies among small firms.

The Labor and Policy Implications of New Technology

At a time of cyclical stress and structural change in the economy, it is inevitable that attention be given in policy and media circles to issues of job potential for the future. Given the traditional definition of technological change as the substitution of capital for labor, it is also inevitable that job displacement be a central focus of attention at this time. Congress's Office of Technology Assessment, for example, recently launched a study entitled "Technology and Structural Unemployment: Retraining Adult Displaced Workers." The costs and benefits of employment policy are destined to be of central concern to government for at least the rest of the decade.

Recent projections by the Bureau of Labor Statistics suggest that the high technology industries will account for only a small proportion of new jobs through 1995.[33] Employment in the high tech sectors increased faster than all wage and salary employment between 1972 and 1982, and BLS projections indicate that this will continue to be the case through 1995. Between 23 and 29 million new jobs will be created between 1982 and 1995, and between 1 and 4.6 million of these jobs are projected to be in the high tech industries; that is, most new jobs will be in other sectors. "Displaced workers and others seeking jobs, and governmental and community organizations seeking to attract jobs to their regions, would be well advised not to limit their search to high tech industries only."[34]

One major factor that is destined to hamper the ability of high tech industries to provide jobs for displaced workers is the *occupational composition* of many high tech industries. They are significantly different from other manufacturing industries that have suffered in recent years, resulting in a "mismatch" problem between the supply and demand for labor. Furthermore, workers in the technology-oriented occuptions generally need specialized post–high school education in some field of technology, with a rigorous high school preparation in science and mathematics as a prerequisite. BLS also examined the distribution of high technology employment in three key states—California, Michigan, and Texas—and found that most jobs were located in the largest metropolitan areas: Los Angeles, San Jose, Dallas, Houston, and Detroit in these particular states.

Another issue getting considerable attention is the impact of factory automation, particularly robotics, on the labor market. Many believe that the "steel-collar worker'' will have a major impact on the U.S. labor force, leading to the elimination of around 1 million factory jobs by 1990, according to one estimate by researchers at Carnegie Mellon University. A study entitled "Robotics and the Economy" by the staff of the Joint Economic Committee has a more optimistic outlook.[35] It estimates the number of jobs that could be performed by robots in 1990 at less than 10 percent and probably less than 5 percent of all jobs. For workers displaced by robots, the JEC study suggests that almost all would be spared unemployment because of retraining and retirement. It also sees robot production as having a positive effect on real economic growth, and hence total employment, in the long run. In this regard it is fairly easy to ignore the job-creation potential of the robotics industry, leading to a postive job multiplier in computing equipment, electronics, and particularly service sectors like software.

Regional differentials in the process of job creation and displacement due to factory automation are not known to date, though undoubtedly some will exist. The concentration of the machinery industries in the industrial Midwest and the Great Lakes states makes it feasible to suggest that this area in particular will be prone to a high degree of structural unemployment in the future. The continued introduction of computerized numerical control of machinery in the Midwest (see Table 3.10) is one factor that will effect job displacement in that region. Indeed, it has been suggested that the critical shortage of skilled labor even in the industrial Midwest will serve as an incentive for companies to continue their automation plans during expansionary phases of the economy.

A study of federal options toward displaced workers by the Congressional Budget Office examines two alternative forms of federal aid: readjustment services to help workers adapt to changed labor markets, and income assistance.[36] Readjustment services would include job-search assistance, training, and relocation aid, policy options also examined recently by the National Academy of Sciences' Committee on National Urban Policy in its initiative to rethink urban policy.[37] In its review of various strategies for increasing worker mobility, the National Academy Committee looked at the need to establish a national job information system and a displaced worker relocation program. The Canadian Job Bank System was viewed as one example of a well-designed mobility assistance program. A national policy on labor mobility that facilitates the matching of workers and jobs and reduces barriers to worker mobility was therefore one major recommendation of the National Academy Committee on Urban Policy. Other recommendations include:

1. sectoral policies or strategies that encourage capital to flow to the more efficient economic sectors,
2. policies that promote the maintenance of urban infrastructure,
3. policies that encourage private investment in activities that accelerate transitions in local economies, and

4. policies that promote investments in urban education systems to improve both basic skills and continuing education to maintain a labor force that can adapt more readily to continuing changes in the economy.

In this regard the National Academy Committee took a broad definition of urban policy: "Ultimately, urban policy should not be a discrete package of programs—a shopping list of federal grants and loans—but rather a long term strategic perspective on a wide range of public policies at each level of government."[38] This also seems to be the appropriate policy context in which to monitor the links between technological change and urban regional development as the national economy continues to change in coming years.

CONCLUSION

This chapter has reviewed some conceptual and empirical issues relating high technology development to regional change in the United States in recent years. While many still disagree on the definition of what constitutes high technology industry, a number of recent studies allow us to map out the spatial incidence of high technology development across the United States. The location of R&D facilities has historically been concentrated in large metropolitan areas, particularly in the Northeast and North Central regions, but this pattern seems to be changing in recent years.

The distribution of high technology jobs across the various regions of the country is seen to correspond relatively closely to the pattern for all industries, but some regional contrasts are evident. While the Northeast and North Central regions have a greater absolute share of high technology industries, growth rates are higher in the states of the South and West. It is generally assumed that a large agglomeration effect exists in the formation of high technology businesses, but no measurable association of high tech business formations was found with the local employment share of high tech industries. Employment growth in high tech firms was seen, however, to be highly responsive to variations in the strength of the local economy and in the supply of technically skilled labor. One study attempts to explain the location factors behind the complex, dispersed pattern of high tech jobs around the country, using a large number of variables; the results however, only confirm the complexity of the situation and the difficulties of explaining high tech location patterns without approaching the problem at a highly disaggregated level. Hence, there is much more that we need to learn about the locational determinants of specific high tech industries.

Recent findings on the spread of new production processes in the U.S. machinery industry show that older plants are more likely to adopt new technologies than newer plants. These results reflect the retooling that has been going on in one of the key capital goods industries of the nation, and much of this is concentrated in the northeastern and midwestern parts of the country. Since adoption rates for new technologies are lower for small firms in regions further removed from the areas where these technologies were developed, this suggests that state policy makers in particular should consider a technology transfer program to encourage the spread of new technologies among small firms. Such an industrial extension service would complement the moves by most states to lure in new high technology–based firms.

Though recent studies suggest that high tech industries will account for only a small proportion of new jobs in the next ten years, policy makers at both federal and state levels need to pay more attention to new labor training and retraining programs to upgrade the technological capabilities of particular areas.

NOTES

1. Joseph A. Schumpeter, *Capitalism, Socialism and Democracy* (New York: Harper & Row, 1942).

2. See Robert Solow, "Technical Change and the Aggregate Production Function," *Review of Economics and Statistics* 39 (1957): 312–20; and Nathan Rosenberg, *Technology and American Economic Growth* (New York: Harper & Row, 1972), 8.

3. See Edwin Mansfield, *Industrial Research and Technological Innovation: An Econometric Analysis* (New York: W.W. Norton, 1968); *Research and Innovation in the Modern Corporation* (New York: W.W. Norton, 1972); *The Production and Application of New Industrial Technology* (New York: W.W. Norton, 1977); Bela Gold, *Research, Technological Change and Economic Analysis* (Lexington, Mass.: D.C. Heath, 1977); Richard R. Nelson and Sydney A. Winter, "In Search of a Useful Theory of Innovation," *Research Policy* 6 (1977), 36–76; and James Utterback, "The Dynamics of Product and Process Innovations in Industry," in C.T. Hill and J.M. Utterback, *Technological Innovation for a Dynamic Economy* (New York: Pergamon Press, 1979), pp. 40-65.

4. See M.I. Kamien and N.L. Schwartz, "Market Structure and Innovation, A Survey," *Journal of Economic Literature* 13 (1976): 1–37.

5. Mansfield, *Industrial Research*, 176.

6. National Science Board, *Science Indicators 1976* (Washington, D.C.: U.S. Government Printing Office, 1976).

7. T. Levitt, "Innovative Imitation," *Harvard Business Review* (Sept. 1966): 65. For a cogent review of the literature on this topic see Louis A. Tornatzky et. al., *The Process of Technological Innovation: Review of the Literature* (Washington, D.C.: National Science Foundation, 1982).

8. See the review by Edward J. Malecki, "Technology and Regional Development: A Survey," *International Regional Science Review* 8 (1983): 89–126. Some of the early ideas in this area were developed by Morgan D. Thomas, "Regional Economic Growth: Some Conceptual Problems," *Land Economics* 45 (1969), 43–51, and in Thomas, "Growth Pole Theory, Technological Change and Regional Economic Growth," *Papers of the Regional Science Association* 34 (1975): 3–25.

9. Raymond Oakey, Alfred Thwaites, and Peter Nash, "The Regional Distribution of Innovation Manufacturing Establishments in Britain," *Regional Studies* 14 (1980): 235–54.

10. U.S. Congress, Office of Technology Assessment, *Technology, Innovation, and Regional Economic Development: Encouraging High Technology Development*, Background Paper No. 2 (Washington, D.C.: U.S. Government Printing Office, 1984), 2.

11. Three recent studies that discuss definitional problems in depth are: Catherine Armington,

C. Harris, and M. Odle, *Formation and Growth in High Technology Industries: A Regional Assessment* (Washington, D.C.: Brookings Institution, 1983); Amy Glasmeir, P. Hall, and A. Markusen, *Recent Evidence on High Technology Industries Spatial Tendencies: A Preliminary Investigation*, Working Paper No. 417 (Berkeley: University of California Institute of Urban and Regional Development, 1983); and Alan W. Riche, D.E. Hecker, and J.U. Burgan, "High Technology Today and Tomorrow: A Small Slice of the Employment Pie," *Monthly Labor Review* (Nov. 1983): 50–58.

12. Riche, Hecker, and Burgan, "High Technology Today."

13. Edward J. Malecki, "Dimensions of R and D Location in the United States," *Research Policy* 9 (1980): 2–22, and "Public and Private Sector Interrelationships, Technological Change, and Regional Development," *Papers of the Regional Science Association* 47 (1981): 121-137.

14. National Science Foundation, *Research and Development by Industry* (Washington, D.C.: Surveys of Science Resources Service, 1982), 22.

15. Malecki, "Dimensions of R and D Location" and "Public and Private Sector Interrelationships."

16. Malecki, "Dimensions of R and D Location," 19.

17. Malecki, "Public and Private Sector Interrelationships."

18. Lynne E. Brown, "Can High Tech Save the Great Lake States," *New England Economic Review* (Nov.-Dec. 1983) 19-33.

19. Armington, Harris, and Odle, *Formation and Growth*.

20. Niles Hansen, "The New International Division of Labor and Manufacturing Decentralization in the United States," *Review of Regional Studies* 9 (1980): 1–11.

21. John Rees, "Technological Change and Regional Shifts in American Manufacturing," *Professional Geographer* 31 (1979): 45–54

22. Glasmeier, Hall, and Markusen, *Recent Evidence on High Technology*.

23. Glasmeier, Hall, and Markusen, *Recent Evidence on High Technology*, 13.

24. Glasmeier, Hall, and Markusen, *Recent Evidence on High Technology*, 46.

25. Nancy Dorfman, Rowe 128: The development of a regional high technology economy, *Research Policy* (1983): 229-316; and Annalee Sayenian, *The Urban Contradictions of Silicon Valley: Regional Growth and the Restructuring of the Semiconductor Industry*, Working Paper (Berkeley: University of California Institute for Urban and Regional Development, 1981).

26. John Rees and Howard A. Stafford, *A Review of Regional Growth and Industrial Location Theory: Towards Understanding the Development of High-Technology Complexes in the U.S.*, paper prepared by the U.S. Congress Office of Technology Assessment, 1983.

27. Howard A. Stafford, *Principles of Industrial Facility Location* (Atlanta, Ga.: Conway Publications, 1980), 70.

28. U.S. Congress, Joint Economic Committee, *Location of High Technology Firms and Regional Economic Development* (Washington, D.C.: U.S. Government Printing Office, 1982). The sectors were SIC 35, machinery; 36, electric and electronic equipment; 37, transportation; 38, instruments; and 28, chemicals. Indeed, most of the three-digit sectors in Table 3.1 are included in these five sectors.

29. See Mansfield, *Research and Innovation* and *Production and Application*, and Gold, *Research, Technological Change and Economic Analysis*. Some of the more salient work by geographers include Torsten Hagerstrand, *Innovation Diffusion as a Spatial Process* (Chicago: University of Chicago Press, 1952), and Lawrence A. Brown, *Innovation Diffusion: A New Perspective* (New York: Methuen, 1980).

30. John Rees, Ronald Briggs, and Raymond Oakey, "The Adoption of New Technology in the American Machinery Industry," *Regional Studies* (Dec. 1984), and John Rees, Ronald Briggs, and Donald Hicks, "New Technology in the American Machinery Industry: Trends and Implications" paper published by the U.S. Congress Joint Economic Committee (Washington, D.C.: U.S. Government Printing Office, 1984).

31. Charles R. Hulten, *The Age Structure of Regional Plant Equipment: Facts and Implications*

of the Reagan Tax Cuts (Washington, D.C.: Urban Institute, 1982), 15.

32. Rees, Briggs, and Hicks, 1984.

33. Riche, Hecker, and Burgar, "High Technology Today."

34. Riche, Hecker, and Burgar, "High Technology Today," 54.

35. U.S. Congress, Joint Economic Committee, *Robotics and the Economy* (Washington, D.C.: U.S. Government Printing Office, 1982).

36. U.S. Congress, Congressional Budget Office, *Dislocated Workers: Issues and Federal Options* (Washington, D.C.: U.S. Government Printing Office, 1982).

37. Royce Hanson, ed., *Rethinking Urban Policy: Urban Development in an Advanced Economy* (Washington, D.C.: National Academy Press, 1983).

38. Hanson, *Rethinking Urban Policy*, 3.

4

Industrial Location and Regional Development

In Chapters 1 and 2, the extent of interregional migration and employment changes since 1950 is documented in detail. Implicit in these shifts of people and jobs, of course, is a major redistribution of business activity within the United States. Existing firms have moved, set up branch plants, and made acquisitions in the areas of rapid population growth. At the same time, new firms have come into existence throughout the Sunbelt and Mountain states.

This chapter discusses the nature of industrial change and its importance to the growth of the Sunbelt. It also looks at several other factors, such as a favorable business climate, that may be attracting entrepreneurs from other regions and encouraging the formation of new businesses in the South and West.

COMPONENTS OF REGIONAL INDUSTRIAL CHANGE

In Tables 1.5 and 1.6, data from the Bureau of Labor Statistics were used to illustrate changes in the level of total nonagricultural and total manufacturing employment by state and region over time. But neither BLS nor the Bureau of the Census identify the kinds of firms or types of plants involved in employment growth and contraction. To fully understand the process of regional change, data on industrial organization must be analyzed as well.

Regional scientists have long recognized the need to identify industrial change according to the size of company and the nature of the expansion or contraction, for instance, whether firms are relocating, setting up branch plants, acquiring other companies, expanding on site, downsizing, starting up, or closing.

In recent years a number of major firms have moved their corporate headquarters from northern to southern cities. For instance, Coca Cola moved from

New York to Atlanta; Shell Oil from New York to Houston; Mobil Oil from New York to Fairfax, Virginia; National Gypsum from Buffalo to Dallas; American Airlines from New York to Fort Worth. This movement by major corporations has helped to create the notion that industrial migration is playing a major role in the economic growth of the Sunbelt. In fact, migration of firms accounts for a very small percentage of the employment growth in the South and West and a similarly small percentage of the employment losses in the North.

Early documentation of the negligible impact of firm migration on employment shifts appeared in a 1975 study by Peter Allaman and David Birch.[1] Working with data from the Dun and Bradstreet files, the authors tabulated and analyzed employment changes between 1969 and 1972 for 3.5 million firms. Net employment change for each census region was defined as the result of births, deaths, expansions, contractions, in-migration, and out-migration. The results of the survey are summarized in Table 4.1.

As the data indicate, a very small proportion of regional employment change can be attributed to in-migration or out-migration of firms. This is true of both the North, where employment is growing slowly, and the South, where employment is growing rapidly. Births and expansions, by contrast, vary significantly among regions and can be cited as the major causes of differential employment growth.

A 1979 update, examining 5.6 million firms, came to similar conclusions.[2] As Table 4.2 suggests, migration of establishments from one state to another was infinitestimal during each of the three time periods examined. Furthermore, the death and contraction rates showed little regional variation. Most of the regional variation in net job change was due to differences in the rate of job creation (firm births and expansions) rather than variations in the rate of job loss. Birch also found that northern and southern central cities were losing employment at comparable rates.

A more recent study by John Rees supports the observations of Allaman and Birch.[3] Using secondary data, industry surveys, and personal interviews, Rees was able to classify location decisions by manufacturing firms in the Dallas–Fort Worth and Houston metropolitan areas between 1960 and 1975. Manufacturing change was defined as an aggregation of location decisions: on site expansions, new plants (both branches and births), relocations, and acquisitions. Since Texas is one of the most dynamic industrial growth areas in the United States, Rees expected to find that firms from the traditional manufacturing belt had expanded into the region to capture sources of supply and new markets. In fact, Rees found that locally based firms and new firms, as opposed to external sources, accounted for most of the manufacturing growth during the 1960–75 period (see Table 4.3).

In the Dallas–Fort Worth area, new plants (branches and births) accounted for 38 percent of all location decisions, followed by expansions (33 percent), relocations (16 percent), and acquisitions (13 percent). In Houston, by contrast, the most common type of location decision (44 percent) was on site expansion, followed by new plants (34 percent), acquisitions (11 percent), and relocations (11 percent). The differing pattern of industrial growth between Dallas–Fort Worth and Houston is a reflection of a different industrial mix. The dominant industries in Houston's expansions were material-oriented sectors such as chemicals and refining, which tend to be location-sensitive. In the Dallas–Fort Worth area, the electronics and aerospace industries, which tend to be more footloose, spawned numerous new companies.

In another study, Rees examined the headquarters locations of firms setting up branches or making acquisitions in the Dallas-Fort Worth area.[4] As Table 4.4 indicates, 57 percent of the acquisitions between 1967 and 1975 were initiated by companies with headquarters in Dallas–Fort Worth, while 47 percent of the branch plants were set up by locally based companies. These results suggest that the recent growth of the Dallas–Fort Worth area is principally a result of local decision making as opposed to external control.

Rees also examined the backward linkage patterns of a number of Dallas–Fort Worth manufacturers:

> The spatial pattern of backward linkages for 45 plants in the Dallas-Fort Worth area suggests a dependency on the more established manufacturing areas of the United States, the manufacturing belt (that is the Middle Atlantic and East North Central Census divisions) and California which accounted for 42 percent of all inputs. Therefore, just as the American industrial heartland once reached out to such peripheral regions for raw materials, now this maturing industrial area depends on that same heartland for manufactured goods for its own industries.[5]

A more recent study by the U.S. Advisory Commission on Intergovernmental Relations concurs with the Birch and Rees findings.[6] ACIR assembled data from the Duns Market Identifiers file of Dun and Bradstreet to determine how many major manufacturing establishments left one state and relocated in another between 1969 and 1976. ACIR found that 554 major manufacturing firms out of 140,093 examined changed locations over this seven-year period, supporting the contention that both interregional and interstate movements of plants are uncommon. Only the Mideast and Great Lakes regions lost more establishments to another region—the Southeast—than to other states in their own region (see Table 4.5).

The Birch, Rees, and ACIR studies together suggest that the primary cause of rising employment in the Sunbelt has been the expansion of existing firms and the birth of new firms. Actual migration of firms, in the sense of leaving one region of the country and reestablishing operations in another, accounts for an extremely small fraction of both employment growth and employment decline. An important implication of these findings, of course, is that economic growth in the South and West does not necessarily imply a decline in the North.

TABLE 4.1
Average Employment Change for All States by Industry and Region, 1970–72 (In Percent)

Area	Net Change	Births	Deaths	Expansion	Contraction	In-migration	Out-migration
			Agriculture				
Northeast	0.8	1.7	-4.2	20.1	-16.6	0.0	-0.1
North Central	0.6	6.0	-10.0	18.4	-13.4	0.2	-0.6
South	-1.9	5.8	-10.6	16.0	-15.2	2.3	-0.0
West	-5.8	5.0	-11.4	16.5	-15.8	0.0	-0.1
			Manufacturing				
Northeast	-12.4	2.7	-12.8	8.0	-10.3	0.4	-0.5
North Central	-8.2	2.2	-10.0	8.7	-0.1	0.1	-0.2
South	-5.6	4.2	-12.2	11.3	-9.0	0.3	-0.1
West	-9.7	4.3	-14.3	12.0	-11.7	0.2	-0.2
			Other Industry				
Northeast	-4.1	5.2	-11.3	14.5	-12.5	0.3	-0.4
North Central	-5.2	5.2	-11.2	14.0	-13.1	0.2	-0.2
South	0.2	8.3	-12.4	16.7	-12.4	0.3	-0.3

West	−0.5	6.0	−12.0	17.2	−11.8	0.1	−0.1

Trade

Northeast	2.1	9.2	−15.0	15.4	−7.5	0.4	−0.4
North Central	5.1	11.4	−15.0	16.5	−7.8	0.1	−0.1
South	7.1	13.2	−15.2	16.8	−7.7	0.2	−0.2
West	5.8	12.8	−18.2	18.5	−7.4	0.1	−0.1

Service

Northeast	−1.0	3.8	−7.4	12.1	−9.2	0.4	−0.7
North Central	−3.3	4.1	−5.9	12.2	−7.3	0.5	−0.2
South	4.1	6.6	−7.7	13.7	−8.7	0.5	−0.2
West	1.1	5.9	−9.1	15.4	−11.3	0.3	−0.1

Total

Northeast	−6.3	4.6	−12.2	11.2	−9.8	0.4	−0.5
North Central	−3.2	4.9	−10.7	11.7	−9.1	0.2	−0.2
South	0.2	7.6	−12.3	14.1	−9.3	0.3	−0.2
West	−1.9	7.3	−14.1	15.3	−10.5	0.2	−0.1

Source: Peter A. Allaman and David L. Birch, *Components of Employment Change for States by Industry Group, 1970–72* (Cambridge, Mass.: Harvard/MIT Joint Center for Urban Studies, 1975).

TABLE 4.2
Annual Rate of Employment Change for States by Growth Rate[a] of State

State Growth Rate	Births	Deaths	Expansion	Contraction	In-migration	Out-migration
			1969–72			
Fast	7.5	5.6	6.2	2.7	0.1	0.03
Moderate	6.0	5.2	4.7	2.8	0.2	0.03
Slow	4.5	4.8	4.0	2.9	0.03	0.03
Decline	3.9	5.1	3.4	3.2	0.2	0.1
U.S. Average	5.6	5.2	4.7	2.9	0.1	0.03
			1972–74			
Fast	6.5	4.6	5.8	2.5	0.1	0.05
Moderate	5.0	4.4	5.0	2.7	0.05	0.05

Slow	4.3	4.6	4.5	2.9	0.2	0.1
Decline	—	—	—	—	—	—
U.S. Average	5.5	4.5	5.3	2.6	0.1	0.05
			1974–76			
Fast	9.5	5.7	5.4	3.1	0.2	0.05
Moderate	6.9	5.3	4.4	3.3	0.1	0.1
Slow	6.2	6.1	4.4	3.5	0.1	0.1
Decline	4.5	5.4	3.6	3.8	0.2	0.1
U.S. Average	6.7	5.7	4.4	3.4	0.1	0.1

[a]The four classes of employment change are: Fast (over 4 percent per year), Moderate (2 to 4 percent per year), Slow (0 to 2 percent per year) and Decline (less than 0 percent per year). On the average, this breakdown divides states into four roughly equal groups, although the size of the groups in any particular year is sensitive to the business cycle.

Source: David L. Birch, *The Job Generation Process* (Cambridge, Mass.: MIT, Program on Neighborhood Change, 1979), 22.

TABLE 4.3
Location Decisions by SIC Group, 1960–75

SIC Group	Food 20	Textiles 22	Apparel 23	Lumber 24	Furniture 25	Paper 26	Printing 27	Chemicals 28	Petroleum 29	Plastics 30	Stone, clay, etc. 32	Primary metals 33	Fabricated metals 34	Machinery 35	Electronics 36	Transport equipment 37	Scientific instruments 38	Miscellaneous 39	N
								Dallas–Fort Worth											
Expansions	94[a]	7	55	15	54	27	54	68	4	52	48	83	128	138	87	105	9	19	997 (33%)
New	73	10	79	47	54	40	56	69	9	85	53	14	128	144	89	101	46	49	1146 (38%)
Acquisitions	46	11	9	9	8	15	32	17	11	10	12	5	61	51	48	26	6	5	382 (13%)

Relocations	22	4	38	17	23	16	28	36	7	19	20	15	69	58	51	26	11	20	480 (16%)
Location Quotients 1972	1.05	—	1.2	0.6	1.1	0.7	1.2	0.6	0.6	0.6	1.1	0.2	0.8	1.0	1.8	2.0	0.3	0.3	8

Houston

Expansions	82	8	4	10	12	27	39	361	38	48	39	83	224	161	52	14	21	11	1234 (44%)
New	39	5	16	28	25	15	75	157	25	40	51	41	186	129	65	25	21	31	974 (34%)
Acquisitions	22	2	2	10	6	5	20	43	4	15	11	11	63	54	39	6	6		319 (11%)
Relocations	10	2	11	6	8	9	31	23	4	11	12	9	59	61	16	7	16	9	303 (11%)
Location Quotients 1972	1.0	—	0.1	0.3	0.4	0.5	0.6	3.5	7.1	0.4	1	0.7	1.3	1.2	0.5	0.1	0.3	0.4	

aItalic figures refer to dominant SIC sectors.

Source: John Rees, "Regional Shifts in the U.S. and the Internal Generation of Manufacturing in Growth Centers of the Southwest," in William C. Wheaton, ed., *Interregional Movements and Regional Growth*, (Washington, D.C.: Urban Institute, 1979), 66–67.

TABLE 4.4
Headquarters Locations of Firms Setting Up Branches and Acquisitions in Dallas–Fort Worth, 1967–75

State	Number of Branches	Number of Acquisitions	Manufacturing Value Added, 1972 (thousands)
California	20	14	$31,195
New York	15	15	30,404
Connecticut	8	2	6,828
Illinois	7	14	25,849
Indiana	6	4	14,112
Ohio	5	6	27,171
Missouri	5	1	8,169
New Jersey	4	7	16,409
Michigan	4	5	23,376
Rhode Island	3	2	1,764
Wisconsin	3	2	9,443
Minnesota	2	6	5,524
Pennsylvania	1	4	23,519
North Carolina	2	2	2,647
Dallas–Fort Worth	102	176	
Rest of Texas	12	35	

Source: John Rees, "Regional Shifts in the U.S. and the Internal Generation of Manufacturing in Growth Centers of the Southwest," in William C. Wheaton, ed., *Interregional Movements and Regional Growth* (Washington, D.C.: Urban Institute, 1979), 51–74.

STATE AND LOCAL INFLUENCES ON INDUSTRIAL LOCATION AND REGIONAL DEVELOPMENT

Most research into domestic economic development conducted over the past several decades has found little evidence to support the significance of state and local government incentives for inducing private investment.[7] Nonetheless, state and local governments apparently believe they have the means, through either legislative action or persuasion, to influence the level of economic activity within their borders. This is evidenced by the fact that tax-free state and local revenue bond financing is offered to industry in forty-five states; twenty-nine states offer other types of low-interest loans; twenty-five states do not collect sales taxes on newly purchased industrial equipment; thirty-eight do not levy inventory taxes on goods in transit; virtually all states have industrial development agencies; and

TABLE 4.5

Classification of Interstate Moves of Major Manufacturing Establishments (1976 Location and 1969 Location)

Regions	Total Gain for States in Region Due to Inter-state Moves	Total Loss for States in Region Due to Inter-state Moves	Intra-regional/ Inter-state Moves	Interregional Moves New England	Mideast	Great Lakes	Plains	South-east	South-west	Rocky Mountains	Far West	Total	Exhibit: Estimated Number of Major Manufacturing Establishments 1969
New England	79	60	36	—	5	3	0	12	0	0	4	24	10,051
Mideast	70	226	48	34	—	18	4	88	11	0	23	178	35,897
Great Lakes	61	125	29	5	10	—	10	41	14	8	8	96	28,918
Plains	31	34	12	1	0	4	—	8	4	1	4	22	9,902
Southeast	181	34	18	2	2	3	2	—	4	1	2	16	21,907
Southwest	49	20	6	1	0	1	2	6	—	2	2	14	9,847
Rocky Mountain	19	4	1	0	0	1	0	0	2	—	0	3	2,736
Far West[a]	64	51	21	0	5	2	1	8	8	6	—	30	20,835
Totals	554	554	171	43	22	32	19	163	43	18	43	383	140,093

Note: Establishments classified in Standard Industrial Classification (SIC) codes 20, 22–39, 48, and 73, having twenty or more employees.
[a] "Far West" includes Alaska and Hawaii.
Source: ACIR ACCESS file.

many state and local governments offer tax credits, abatements, and rapid depreciation to encourage new investment in plant and equipment.

Why do state and local governments offer these incentives? Presumably, the objective is to improve that state's "business climate" on the assumption that economic development—defined as new investment and job creation—is more likely to occur where the "business climate" is favorable than where it is unfavorable.

Defining a Favorable "Business Climate"

The notion of a "business climate" is necessarily ambiguous. It means different things to different groups. To a locational consultant, the business climate may be a buzz-word relating to a particular legislative action, such as a tax concession or restrictive labor law, that is viewed as probusiness. To a corporate executive involved in site selection, the business climate may be viewed in terms of the attitudes of public officials toward new business development or the availability and productivity of skilled and unskilled labor. To the development administration of a state or local government, the business climate may connote the availability of industrial revenue bond financing, tax incentives, and other promotional activities.

Similarly, the dynamics of growth cannot be completely quantified or modeled. A business executive's decision to locate in, expand, or leave a particular site may not be based on purely economic considerations. The subjective elements may be as important as the objective factors in the decision-making process. Perceptions may be as important as facts.

Several recent analyses have attempted to construct an objective basis for measuring the business climate. These studies help to illustrate the contrasting views as to what constitutes a favorable environment for industrial expansion. They also provide a basis for reassessing the impact of state and local tax incentives on regional economic development.

The Fantus Study

In 1975, the Fantus Company, a locational consulting firm that is a subsidiary of Dun and Bradstreet, developed a business climate ranking for all forty-eight contiguous states at the behest of the Illinois Manufacturers Assoication.[8] Fantus based its business climate ranking on fifteen factors deemed important to firms considering alternative states as a possible location:

1. corporate income taxes as a percentage of total state taxes
2. per capita property tax
3. per capita welfare expenditures
4. per capita personal income tax
5. total state taxes per capita

6. total state and local taxes per capita
7. labor legislation favorable to management
8. legal coverage relative to strikes, picketing, and boycotts
9. regulation of labor unions
10. unemployment compensation tax rate
11. average workers' compensation payment
12. governmental units per 1,000 population
13. state and local payroll per capita
14. per capita state debt
15. per capita state and local debt.

All forty-eight contiguous states were ranked in each category relative to one another. If a state ranked 1–12 relative to other states in a particular category it was rated excellent; 13–24, good; 25–36, fair; and 37–48, poor. The criteria for excellence included low taxes, low levels of public assistance, restrictive labor legislation, and a low level of government spending and debt.

Each state's ranking in each category was summed to arrive at a composite score. The lower the composite, the higher the overall business climate ranking. The twelve best and twelve worst states for business climate, along with their composite scores, were as follows:

The Best		*The Worst*	
Texas	192	New York	628
Alabama	210	California	581
Virginia	214	Massachusetts	547
South Dakota	230	Michigan	532
South Carolina	236	Delaware	520
North Carolina	239.5	Connecticut	516.5
Florida	244	Pennsylvania	506
Arkansas	248	Minnesota	505.5
Indiana	251	Oregon	499
Utah	279	Washington	495
North Dakota	286	Vermont	489
Mississippi	287	New Jersey	483

Eleven of the fifteen factors evaluated by Fantus were directly or indirectly a consequence of state tax and spending policies. Also of note, among the top twelve states in the Fantus ranking, all but Indiana have right-to-work laws.

The Alexander Grant Studies

Since 1979, Alexander Grant & Company has conducted an annual study of general manufacturing business climates of the forty-eight contiguous states in cooperation with the Conference of State Manufacturers' Association (COSMA).[9] The studies rank each of the states on twenty-two measurement factors that manufacturers agree represent the attractiveness of states to their business. The factors are oriented toward the cost of doing business and the availability of important resources. Differences among states, as measured by these factors, reflect their relative attractiveness to manufacturing operations.

Many of the factors evaluated by Alexander Grant are similar to those in the Fantus study. The major difference is that the Grant studies look at changes in state taxes, spending, wages, and so on in addition to absolute levels. Furthermore, separate rankings for government and nongovernment controlled factors are calculated.

As Table 4.6 suggests, there is a fairly good correlation between the Alexander Grant business climate ranking for 1982 and the number of manufacturing jobs won or lost between 1970 and 1981. Among the top twelve states in the business climate ranking, all showed sizeable manufacturing job increases, while eight of the twelve "worst" states showed job losses.

The Cornell Study

In 1976, the New York State School of Industrial and Labor Relations at Cornell University completed a survey that highlights some important dimensions to the business environment not considered in the Fantus or Alexander Grant reports.[10]

Through cogitation and literature review, NYSSILR came up with a list of fifty-eight factors affecting the business climate. The list included taxes, labor supply, availability of tax concessions, attitudes of public officials, energy supplies, transportation, proximity to markets, weather, recreational and cultural resources, and many other conditions deemed important in site selection.

A questionnaire was sent to a sample of large employers in New York State. Three hundred eighteen responses were received, evenly divided between upstate and downstate. About three-fifths of the replies were from goods-producing firms and two-fifths from service-producing firms. In each case the company's chief executive or another high-level corporate official completed the questionnaire.

Respondents were asked, among other things, to indicate which five of the fifty-eight factors were most important to them in selecting a site in which to locate or expand. The results are summarized in Table 4.7.

Far and away the most important factor was deemed to be the supply of skilled labor. Second was proximity to markets, followed by productivity of the labor force, supply of unskilled labor, and the level of state *personal* income tax. In short, human resources and location were deemed much more important than business taxes or incentives in the site selection process.

As mentioned earlier, virtually all states provide assorted packages of sub-

TABLE 4.6
Business Climate Ranking and Change
in Manufacturing Employment, 1970–81

1982 Rank	State	Change in Manufacturing Employment: 1970–81 (thousands)	Percent Change, 1970–81
1	Florida	144.9	45.1
2	Texas	366.5	49.5
3	North Carolina	48.9	13.8
4	North Dakota	5.4	54.5
5	South Carolina	48.2	14.2
6	Georgia	54.3	11.7
7	Arizona	68.4	75.0
8	Nebraska	10.0	11.8
9	Mississippi	39.6	21.8
10	Kansas	53.4	39.7
11	Idaho	12.0	29.8
12	Louisiana	44.7	25.5
13	Tennessee	42.1	9.1
14	South Dakota	10.0	63.3
15	Colorado	66.9	56.9
16	Nevada	12.0	142.9
17	Virginia	47.8	13.1
18	Arkansas	42.5	25.3
19	Missouri	−16.1	−3.6
20	Utah	34.4	62.4
21	New Hampshire	24.6	26.8
22	Wyoming	2.7	36.5
23	Alabama	42.2	13.0
24	Oklahoma	64.9	48.5
25	Montana	−0.4	−1.7
26	California	560.8	36.0
27	Maryland	−40.1	−14.8
28	Vermont	10.3	25.4
29	Indiana	−53.3	−7.5
30	Kentucky	19.2	7.6
31	New Mexico	13.1	62.4
32	Minnesota	32.9	10.3
33	Massachusetts	18.5	2.9
34	New Jersey	−92.0	−10.7
35	Iowa	20.4	9.5
36	Wisconsin	42.2	8.4

TABLE 4.6 (continued)

1982 Rank	State	Change in Manufacturing Employment: 1970–81 (thousands)	Percent Change, 1970–81
37	Washington	62.5	26.1
38	Connecticut	−6.5	−1.5
39	West Virginia	−15.1	−11.9
40	Maine	2.4	2.2
41	Delaware	−0.3	−0.4
42	Illinois	−207.2	−15.4
43	Oregon	31.0	18.0
44	Ohio	−174.9	−12.4
45	New York	−328.6	−18.7
46	Pennsylvania	−223.7	−14.7
47	Rhode Island	5.4	4.5
48	Michigan	−93.9	−8.8

Sources: U.S. Department of Labor, Bureau of Labor Statistics, *Employment and Earnings Historical Data, 1936–1982* (Washington, D.C.: U.S. G.P.O., 1984); Alexander Grant & Co., *General Manufacturing Business Climates, 1983* (Chicago, Alexander Grant & Co., 1984).

sidized loans, tax credits, and tax forgiveness to encourage investment in new plant and equipment. But it is unlikely that any of these "incentives" can alter the five critical factors in the locational calculus cited by the Cornell study. Indeed, the patterns of regional economic growth and business development would probably not look much different in the absence of the existing plethora of developmental incentives.

Taken as a whole, these incentives represent a serious misallocation of resources. In the main, government is subsidizing firms for undertaking investments that would likely have been made in any case. Furthermore, when one considers that any incentive designed to reduce a company's state or local tax bill will increase that firm's federal tax liability—due to the deductibility of state and local taxes in computing federal net taxable income—the superfluity of fiscal incentives becomes even more apparent.

Fiscal Pressures and Economic Growth

Although tax inducements to businesses may be an insignificant factor in industrial location and expansion, the overall level and structure of state and local taxes can be a strong influence on the economic performance of a given region. In fact, a relatively low level of state and local taxes may be one of the

TABLE 4.7
The 18 Factors Most Often Selected by Businesspeople
as Most Important in Locating a Firm
(Each of 318 Respondents Listed Up to 5 Factors)

Factors	Number of Times Listed and Order of Listing						Weighted Total[a]
	Total	1st	2nd	3rd	4th	5th	
Supply of skilled labor	120	82	14	7	10	7	514
Proximity to markets	80	25	13	14	16	12	263
Productivity of labor force	77	11	29	24	6	7	262
Supply of unskilled labor	68	20	32	4	9	3	261
Level of state individual income tax	62	13	10	13	15	11	185
Level of wages/benefits	61	11	16	21	11	2	206[b]
Level of state corporate income tax	52	5	7	9	15	16	126
Attitude of organized labor	48	4	15	12	11	6	144[b]
Attitude of state government leaders	48	11	8	4	9	16	133[b]
Access to truck transportation	40	4	5	12	8	11	103
Proximity to raw materials or supplies	38	7	7	11	8	5	117[b]
Attitude of state legislators	29	10	4	4	3	8	92
Level of local property tax	29	3	3	4	12	7	70
Level of state corporate franchise tax	27	4	6	7	7	3	82
Availability of state financial incentives	27	3	5	5	5	9	69
Attitude of local government leaders	27	2	6	2	6	11	63
State unemployment insurance laws	26	7	8	5	5	1	93[b]
Level of county or city sales tax	26	3	1	6	5	11	69

[a]In weighted total, extra weight is given to item depending on order listed by the respondent. If listed first, each mention is given a value of 5; for second, 4; for third, 3; for fourth, 2; for fifth, 1.

[b]If weighted total is used for ranking, these items move up in rating.

Source: F.F. Foltman, *Business Climate in New York State: Perceptions of Labor and Management Officials* (Ithaca, N.Y.: New York State School of Industrial and Labor Relations, 1976).

key reasons that the Sunbelt and Mountain states are gaining population and industry faster than other regions. Several studies point to this conclusion.

A report by the Southern Regional Education Board suggests that the economic gains in the South are linked to the region's underutilized tax potential.[11] According to the study, in 1975 state and local governments in the South used only 82.5 percent of their tax potential—defined as the national average tax collection rate. Further, the taxes that accounted for most of the underutilization were those on property and personal income as opposed to taxes on business. By contrast, the Middle Atlantic states were found to have an overutilization rate of 10.1 percent; the overutilization rate for New York State alone was 34 percent. If New York had collected taxes at the average national rates in 1975, its total take would have been reduced by $4.8 billion.

The U.S. Advisory Commission on Intergovernmental Relations has also intimated that high and rising state and local tax burdens in some states may be influencing industrial location and interregional migration:

> Both the citizens of the state and multistate corporations are more likely to perceive a heavier burden in those states where tax burdens are rising than in those states where taxes as a percentage of income are either remaining relatively constant or falling. It is that *perceived* pressure which may help to account for some of the resistance on the part of the taxpayer to increase the size of the public sector and the reluctance of corporations to locate in certain areas. . . . With the exception of Hawaii, California, Nevada, and West Virginia, all of the states in the relatively high and rising (tax) category are in New England, the Mideast, and the Great Lakes region, while about half the Sunbelt states are in the relatively low and falling group.[12]

The data in Table 4.8 tend to support the notion that the fastest-growing states are those with relatively low and falling tax burdens. Expressing the state and local tax burden as a percentage of state personal income, and comparing the years 1953 and 1981, one sees that those states with above-average increases in tax burdens were generally the slowest growing in terms of per capita income. Conversely, those states with declining relative tax burdens, located primarily in the Sunbelt, were the fastest growing as measured by per capita income changes between 1950 and 1980.

A recent study by Harris Bank of Chicago presents further evidence on the impact of relative tax burdens on state economic development.[13] The major conclusions of this study were: (1) a state's relative economic growth was loosely related to the change in a state's relative tax burden, with those states displaying above-average increases in their tax burden tending to show below-average economic growth and vice versa and (2) once allowance is made for a three-year period of adjustment to tax changes, there is a strong relationship suggesting that above average increases in a state's tax burden can lead to below-average economic growth down the road.

TABLE 4.8
State and Local Tax Revenue in Relation to
State Personal Income, 1953 and 1981

Region and State	Tax Revenue as a Percent of Personal Income			State Percent Related to U.S. Average (U.S. = 100.0)			Percent Change in Per Capita Income, 1950–80[a]
	1981	1953	Percent Increase	1981	1953	Percent Increase or Decrease (−)	
United States	11.29	7.58	48.9	100.0	100.0	—	536
New England	11.82	7.90	49.6	104.7	104.2	0.5	547
Connecticut	10.20	6.06	68.3	90.3	79.9	13.0	527
Maine	11.89	8.95	32.8	105.3	118.1	−10.8	568
Massachusetts	13.28	8.77	51.4	117.6	115.7	1.6	520
New Hampshire	8.68	8.28	4.8	76.9	109.2	−29.6	580
Rhode Island	11.53	7.02	64.2	102.1	92.6	10.3	488
Vermont	12.58	9.62	30.8	111.5	126.9	−12.1	598
Mideast	13.11	7.46	75.7	116.1	98.4	18.0	473
Delaware	10.84	4.21	157.5	96.0	55.5	73.0	385
Maryland	11.24	6.33	77.6	99.6	83.5	19.3	553
New Jersey	11.21	6.59	70.1	99.3	86.9	14.3	496
New York	15.84	8.79	80.2	140.4	116.0	21.0	448
Pennsylvania	10.92	6.17	77.0	96.8	81.4	18.9	512
D.C.	14.69	5.90	149.9	130.1	77.8	67.2	442

TABLE 4.8 (continued)

Region and State	Tax Revenue as a Percent of Personal Income			State Percent Related to U.S. Average (U.S. = 100.0)			Percent Change in Per Capita Income, 1950–80[a]
	1981	1953	Percent Increase	1981	1953	Percent Increase or Decrease (−)	
Great Lakes	10.59	6.78	56.2	93.8	89.4	4.9	494
Illinois	11.05	6.37	73.5	97.9	84.0	16.5	476
Indiana	9.23	7.08	30.4	81.8	93.4	−12.4	491
Michigan	11.57	7.31	58.3	102.5	96.4	6.3	485
Ohio	9.20	5.87	56.7	81.5	77.4	5.3	484
Wisconsin	12.24	8.91	37.4	108.5	117.5	− 7.7	533
Plains	10.45	8.25	26.7	92.6	108.8	−14.9	556
Iowa	11.08	9.22	20.2	98.2	121.6	−23.8	530
Kansas	10.03	8.71	15.2	88.9	114.9	−22.6	592
Minnesota	12.00	9.38	27.9	106.3	123.7	−14.1	590
Missouri	8.77	6.14	42.8	77.7	81.0	− 4.1	528
Nebraska	10.37	7.69	34.9	91.9	101.5	− 9.5	529
North Dakota	11.24	11.27	− 0.3	99.6	148.7	−33.0	593
South Dakota	10.85	10.79	0.6	96.2	142.3	−32.4	529
Southeast	10.12	7.86	28.8	89.7	103.7	−13.5	688
Alabama	9.85	7.00	40.7	87.3	92.3	− 5.4	751

Arkansas	9.32	7.92	17.7	82.5	104.5	−21.1	781
Florida	9.34	9.20	1.5	82.8	121.4	−31.8	602
Georgia	10.55	7.67	37.6	93.5	101.2	− 7.6	681
Kentucky	10.32	6.47	59.5	91.5	85.4	7.1	676
Louisians	11.54	10.43	10.6	102.3	137.6	−25.7	655
Mississippi	10.78	9.37	15.1	95.5	123.6	−22.7	772
North Carolina	10.29	8.25	24.7	91.2	108.8	−16.2	654
South Carolina	10.66	8.61	23.8	94.5	113.6	−16.8	714
Tennessee	9.56	7.32	30.6	84.7	96.6	−12.3	677
Virginia	10.05	6.09	65.0	89.0	80.3	10.8	665
West Virginia	10.71	6.81	57.3	94.9	89.8	5.7	632
Southwest	10.56	7.34	43.9	93.6	96.8	− 3.3	608
Arizona	11.49	8.50	35.2	101.8	112.1	− 9.2	561
New Mexico	14.02	8.66	61.9	124.2	114.2	8.8	566
Oklahoma	11.05	9.07	21.8	97.9	119.7	−18.2	698
Texas	10.04	6.68	50.3	89.0	88.1	1.0	608
Rocky Mountain	11.25	8.60	30.8	99.7	113.5	−12.2	512
Colorado	10.20	8.93	14.2	90.3	117.8	−23.3	574
Idaho	10.01	9.00	11.2	88.7	118.7	−25.3	522
Montana	12.87	7.62	68.9	114.0	100.5	13.4	426
Utah	11.89	8.44	40.8	105.3	111.3	− 5.4	484
Wyoming	15.53	8.73	77.9	137.6	115.2	19.4	553
Far West	11.30	8.34	35.5	100.1	110.0	− 9.0	497
California	11.49	8.41	36.6	101.8	110.9	− 8.2	491

TABLE 4.8 (continued)

Region and State	Tax Revenue as a Percent of Personal Income			State Percent Related to U.S. Average (U.S. = 100.0)			Percent Change in Per Capita Income, 1950–80[a]
	1981	1953	Percent Increase	1981	1953	Percent Increase or Decrease (−)	
Nevada	10.26	7.93	29.4	90.9	104.6	−13.1	432
Oregon	11.85	8.24	43.8	105.0	108.7	− 3.4	475
Washington	10.04	8.07	24.4	89.0	106.5	−16.4	516
Alaska	50.02	5.03	894.0	443.1	66.4	567.3	436
Hawaii	13.75	8.23	67.1	121.8	108.6	−12.2	629

[a]Figures represent unweighted averages of states in regional groups.

Sources: Advisory Commission on Intergovernmental Relations, *Significant Features of Fiscal Federalism* (Washington, D.C.: U.S. G.P.O., 1976) 45–56; U.S. Department of Commerce, Bureau of the Census, *Historical Statistics of the United States,* ser. F297–348, 1975, 243–45; *Survey of Current Business* (April 1982), 20.

Data on personal income growth, allowing for a three-year lag, tend to support these conclusions. As indicated in Table 4.9, states with relatively small increases in tax burdens between 1967 and 1974 tended to show above-average increases in personal income between 1970 and 1977. By contrast, many states whose tax burdens increased relative to the nation during the 1967–74 period showed below-average income gains between 1970 and 1977.

High and/or rising state and local tax burdens may impede industrial expansion and encourage out-migration for a variety of reasons. As discussed in Chapter 1, cost-of-living differentials are one of the factors accelerating the migration of people and business to the Sunbelt. A major cause of these differentials in living costs is state and local taxes. A wage earner moving from New York to Texas, for example, will no longer pay a steeply progressive personal imcome tax, and his sales and property tax payments will also drop dramatically.

State and local taxes on persons may also be viewed as a barometer of the business climate and thereby indirectly influence locational decisions. High personal taxes in many northern states may be an impediment to business growth since they force up salary scales for executive, managerial, and technical personnel. They may also interfere with estate-building by top management people who actually make locational decisions.

SUMMARY

This chapter has examined several specific influences on regional development: industrial migration, the "business climate," and state and local tax burdens. Actual migration of firms, in the sense of shutting down in one state and reopening in another, was found to be an extremely minor factor in employment growth or decline.

On the other hand, many states projecting a favorable business climate image have been successful in attracting entrepreneurial migrants and have realized substantial employment growth. In the main, the good "business climate" states are found in the Sunbelt and Mountain regions. These states have also shown declining relative state and local tax burdens since 1953, which has been an additional factor encouraging in-migration and rapid industrial growth.

TABLE 4.9
Tax Burden and Personal Income Changes

Relative Tax Burden Changes, 1967 to 1974 Ranked Highest to Lowest	Relative Personal Income Changes, 1970 to 1977 Ranked Lowest to Highest
Relative Tax Burden Growth Greater Than 10% of U.S. Average	*Relative Personal Income Growth Less than 90% of U.S. Average*
1. Washington, D.C.	1. New York
2. Illinois	2. Connecticut
3. Vermont	3. Massachusetts
4. Pennsylvania	4. Washington, D.C.
5. New York	5. Rhode Island
6. Michigan	6. Illinois
7. Rhode Island	7. New Jersey
8. Maine	8. Ohio
9. Massachusetts	9. Delaware
Relative Tax Burden Growth Near U.S. Average	*Relative Personal Income Growth Near U.S. Average*
10. Alaska	10. Pennsylvania
11. New Jersey	11. Vermont
12. Connecticut	12. Maryland
13. Maryland	13. Missouri
14. Nebraska	14. Wisconsin
15. Ohio	15. Indiana
16. Wisconsin	16. Hawaii
17. Georgia	17. Minnesota
18. Virginia	18. California
19. Missouri	19. Maine
20. Indiana	20. Nebraska
21. Minnesota	21. Kansas
22. New Hampshire	22. Michigan
23. Nevada	23. Montana
24. California	24. Washington

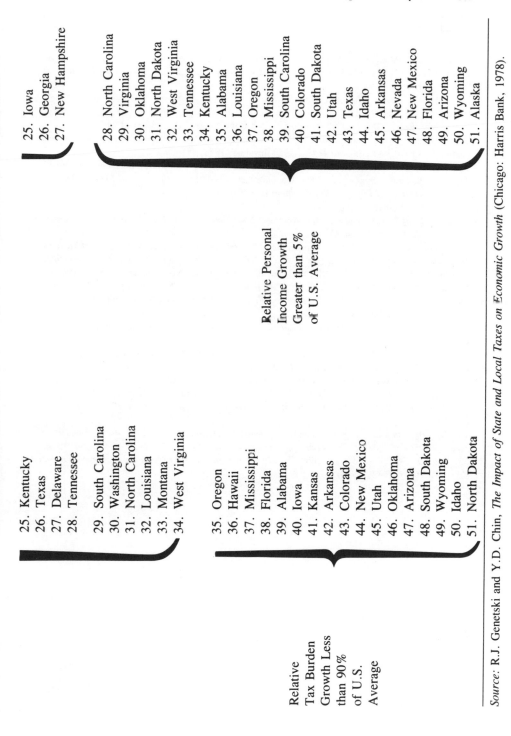

Relative Tax Burden Growth Less than 90% of U.S. Average

25. Kentucky
26. Texas
27. Delaware
28. Tennessee
29. South Carolina
30. Washington
31. North Carolina
32. Louisiana
33. Montana
34. West Virginia
35. Oregon
36. Hawaii
37. Mississippi
38. Florida
39. Alabama
40. Iowa
41. Kansas
42. Arkansas
43. Colorado
44. New Mexico
45. Utah
46. Oklahoma
47. Arizona
48. South Dakota
49. Wyoming
50. Idaho
51. North Dakota

Relative Personal Income Growth Greater than 5% of U.S. Average

25. Iowa
26. Georgia
27. New Hampshire
28. North Carolina
29. Virginia
30. Oklahoma
31. North Dakota
32. West Virginia
33. Tennessee
34. Kentucky
35. Alabama
36. Louisiana
37. Oregon
38. Mississippi
39. South Carolina
40. Colorado
41. South Dakota
42. Utah
43. Texas
44. Idaho
45. Arkansas
46. Nevada
47. New Mexico
48. Florida
49. Arizona
50. Wyoming
51. Alaska

Source: R.J. Genetski and Y.D. Chin, *The Impact of State and Local Taxes on Economic Growth* (Chicago: Harris Bank, 1978).

NOTES

1. Peter A. Allaman and David L. Birch, *Components of Employment Change for States by Industry Group, 1970–72*, Working Paper No. 5 (Cambridge, Mass.: Harvard/MIT Joint Center for Urban Studies, 1975).

2. David L. Birch, *The Job Generation Process* (Cambridge, Mass.: MIT Program on Neighborhood Change, 1979), 21-25.

3. John Rees, "Regional Shifts in the U.S. and the Internal Generation of Manufacturing in Growth Centers of the Southwest," in William C. Wheaton, ed., *Interregional Movements and Regional Growth* (Washington, D.C.: Urban Institute, 1979), 51–74.

4. John Rees, "Manufacturing Change, Internal Control and Government Spending in a Growth Region of the United States," in F.E.I. Hamilton, ed. *Industrial Movement and Change: International Experience and Public Policy* (London: Longman, 1978).

5. Rees, "Manufacturing Change," 14.

6. Advisory Commission on Intergovernmental Relations, *Interstate Tax Competition* (Washington, D.C.: ACIR, 1981), 34–47.

7. For instance, Advisory Commission on Intergovernmental Relations, *State-Local Taxation and Industrial Location* (Washington, D.C.: U.S.G.P.O., 1967) and *Interstate Tax Competition* (Washington D.C.: U.S.G.P.O., 1981); Bernard L. Weinstein, "State Tax Incentives to Promote Private Investment in Urban Poverty Areas: An Evaluation," *Land Economics* (November, 1971): 421–422; Roger J. Vaughan, *State Taxation and Economic Development* (Washington, D.C.: Council of State Planning Agencies, 1979).

8. Fantus Company, *Comparative Business Climate Study* (Chicago: Illinois Manufacturer's Association, 1975).

9. For example, Alexander Grant & Co., *The Fourth Study of General Manufacturing Business Climates* (Chicago: Alexander Grant & Company, 1983).

10. F.F. Foltman, *Business Climate in New York State: Perceptions of Labor and Management Officials* (Ithaca, N.Y.: New York State School of Industrial and Labor Relations, 1976).

11. Southern Regional Education Board, *State and Local Revenue Potential, 1975* (Atlanta, Ga.: SREB, 1977).

12. Advisory Commission of Intergovernmental Relations, *Measuring the Fiscal Blood Pressure of the States, 1964–1974* (Washington, D.C.: U.S.G.P.O., 1977), 2–3.

13. R.J. Genetski and Y.D. Chin, *The Impact of State and Local Taxes on Economic Growth* (Chicago: Harris Bank, 1978).

5

Industrial Policy and
Regional Industrial
Change in the United States

INTRODUCTION

An increasingly important regional issue—although it is not usually recognized as a regional issue *per se*—is that of industrial change. Indeed, industrial change has become a subject of considerable controversy among policy makers, the academic community, and spokespeople for industry and labor, and has given rise to various industrial policy proposals nominally intended to effect a more efficient and equitable distribution of economic resources among competing industrial activities.

Generally, these industrial policy proposals may be broadly categorized as being of a sectoral nature to the extent they tend to focus exclusively on the manufacturing sector or specific industries within the manufacturing sector. Advocates of such policies, for instance, usually argue that many traditional manufacturing industries have been slow to adapt to an increasingly competitive international environment and that an explicit policy is necessary either to make these industries more competitive or to ease the transition to new industries altogether. What is very often ignored, however, is the spatial aspect of the industrial change process. The issue of industrial change is a *regional* issue since the migration of productive resources from a declining industry into a newer, more competitive one also frequently entails the migration of those resources to alternate locations as well. Indeed, it is not merely coincidence that industrial policy proposals have received their greatest support in the traditional manufacturing belt of the Northeast-Midwest and little serious consideration in the Sunbelt states since, to some degree, they offer northern policy makers a means of preserving an eroding manufacturing base and, consequently, the constituencies that guarantee their political careers as well as encouraging the growth of new manufacturing industries that may alleviate or resolve structural unemployment.

Viewed in a slightly different context, industrial policy proposals may be interpreted as efforts to maintain an existing spatial distribution of productive resources by providing mobility for those resources among declining and emerging industries.

The purpose of this chapter is to examine the regional implications of industrial change and, by extension, industrial policy. Following a conceptual overview of the process of industrial change and a brief review of certain representative industrial policy proposals, an empirical examination of structural change within the Texas Gulf Coast rice farming industry and the efficacy of industrial policy as an agent of regional industrial change will be discussed.

It is both useful and interesting to frame a discussion of industrial change and its regional implications in terms of the experience of a specific regional agricultural industry—even through the current debate surrounding the issue has focused almost exclusively on changes in traditional manufacturing industries—given the long history of explicit federal policy intervention in the agricultural sector. Fredrich Hayek recognized the policy relationship between the agricultural and industrial sectors many years ago, long before the current debate over industrial change, when he pointed out that

> in most countries the process of taking agriculture out of the market mechanism and subjecting it to increasing government direction began before the same was done in industry. . . . The tendency was perhaps even stronger in countries where the agricultural population constituted a comparatively small part of the total but, because of a peculiar political position, was given privileges which no similar group had yet attained. . . .[1]

THE TRANSFORMATION OF AN INDUSTRY BY MARKET FORCES

Although industries may be profoundly affected by government intervention, by far the greatest influences upon economic activity involve the complex interaction of market forces. Economic structures—patterns of production, distribution, and consumption—though seemingly static in the short run, are constantly in a state of flux and are eventually modified substantially and even displaced by newer, more efficient structures in response to changing production technologies and tastes of consumers that reveal themselves as shifting structures of supply and demand.

The importance of this phenomenon—the "sweeping away" of old structures—is often discounted or even ignored by proponents of industrial policies that seek to alter the pace or direction of industrial change. In order to properly conceptualize the phenomenon of industrial change and, additionally, to provide an intellectual point of reference for the empirical examination that follows, two highly complementary and explicitly focused theories of industrial change will be reviewed: Joseph Schumpeter's[2] analysis of "creative destruction," and Raymond Vernon's[3] product-cycle theory. Schumpeter, of course, emphasized the role of technological innovation as the driving force of industrial change and, hence, as the very heart of the capitalist system itself. Vernon, building on Schumpeter's identification of the importance of technological innovation, explains industrial change in terms of the life cycle experienced by a product as it responds to changes in production technologies, consumer preferences, and resultant patterns of trade. Seev Hirsch[4] and John Rees[5] have further developed the life cycle hypothesis to explain changes experienced by entire industries and regions.

SCHUMPETER'S PROCESS OF "CREATIVE DESTRUCTION"

As was discussed in Chapter 2, Schumpeter's perspective of capitalist development seems to offer an alternative to the conventional neoclassical paradigm of a "normal" economy that is in static equilibrium. Indeed, for Schumpeter, the central problem of economics was not equilibrium, but the dynamics of disequilibrium reflected in continuous structural change. At the center of an open system in dynamic disequilibrium, Schumpeter placed entrepreneurs and their ability to innovate in response to ever-changing market conditions. It was on this point, in fact, that he departed most strikingly from the economic orthodoxy[6] of his time, which relegated the process of innovation to a relatively minor and insignificant role. It was the entrepreneur, Schumpeter argued, who, as opportunity costs increased, moved economic resources away from inefficient and obsolete activities and into new, more profitable and efficient ones. In fact, although it does not explicitly include the spatial dimension, Schumpeter's notion of innovation as the driving force in capitalism implies a dynamic economy shaped by the locational decisions of entrepreneurs:

> The essential point to grasp is that in dealing with capitalism we are dealing with an evolutionary process. . . . The fundamental impulse that sets and keeps the capitalist engine in motion comes from the new consumers' goods, the new methods of production or transportation, the new markets, the new forms of industrial organization that capitalist enterprise creates.[7]

In other words, Schumpeter argued that the entrepreneur would adapt and innovate in the face of changes in the comparative costs of factors of production or in established patterns of final product demand. To the extent that these phenomena are both a function of, and an influence on, the location of economic activity, Schumpeter's perspective is inherently, though not explicitly, spatially dynamic.

The location-rent differential and industrial change: Before moving on to a discussion of the extension of Schumpeter's work into the development of the product-cycle theory, it is useful to digress briefly to an examination of the location-rent differential as a motivator of industrial change at the micro level. Moreover, since an examination of structural change within the rice farming industry inevitably involves a concern for the transit of land resources among alternative competing uses, a review of the location-rent differential is in order.[8]

The location-rent differential has its origin in Johann von Thunen's *Der isolierte Staat in Beziehung auf Landwirtschaft und Nationalökonomie*.[9] Briefly, Thunen conceived of a town located at the center of a uniformly fertile plain, isolated from the surrounding world by an uncultivated wilderness. By assumption, the town functioned as a central place for a dispersed rural population where marketable agricultural surpluses could be exchanged for manufactured goods and services. The object of Thunen's scheme was the determination of an optimal pattern of cultivation and hence land use. Accordingly, he reasoned that commodities that are heavy or bulky in relation to their value should be produced nearer to the market and potential consumers since it would be comparatively more expensive to supply them from areas farther from the market. Alternatively, commodities that are lighter in relation to their market value should be produced in locations more distant from the market since it would be comparatively less expensive to supply them from areas farther from the market. This reasoning led Thunen to conclude that an optimal pattern of agricultural land use should take the form of concentric rings around the central place, each ring being devoted to the cultivation of a particular commodity. Although this analysis greatly oversimplifies the locational choices of agricultural entrepreneurs, it did give rise to the notion that the production of a good is spatially organized on the basis of the rent, or opportunity costs, associated with a particular form of land utilization.

Placed within the broader Schumpeterian scheme, the location-rent differential is a graphic expression of the process of "creative destruction" and demonstrates the microlevel incentives underlying structural change. The emergence and adoption of new technologies that sweep away obsolete or redundant industrial structures, for example, are reflected in changing location-rent differentials for each industry as the opportunity costs of a particular location tied to a mature technology and production arrangement increase.

VERNON'S LIFE CYCLE HYPOTHESIS

The idea that industrial change is spatially dynamic, however, has been more formally and explicitly developed in Vernon's product cycle theory. The focus of the product cycle theory is the evolution of a product through three distinct stages in its life cycle. Specifically, the product cycle theory holds that, over time, innovations introduced in a particular industry find export markets as incomes abroad rise and as domestic labor costs increase and the industry becomes more capital-intensive. Thus, exports from the industry tend to grow, resulting in a pattern that might be termed the new product stage of the product cycle. In time, however, two factors emerge to influence the newly established trade pattern. First, the demand in some export markets grows sufficiently large to support local production that can exploit the existing scale economies; and, second, the product becomes sufficiently standardized that price competition begins to play an important role. Consequently, the patterned distribution of factors of production lends a spatial dimension to the consideration of costs. This pattern has been termed the "maturing product" stage. At this stage competing producers are likely to appear, as government policies, shipping costs, and lower factor costs shift advantage to alternative locations for production arrangements and sales outside the producing region. Eventually, the output of competing regions becomes price competitive within the domestic market of the original producer, so that a region that formerly exported a particular commodity may find itself importing it. This final phase of the product cycle has been called the "standardized product" stage.

The new product stage of the product cycle is typically characterized by a primitive, labor-intensive production technology that inhibits rapid industry growth. Because this stage represents the link between the phasing out of an old, obsolete technology and the emergence of a new one, economies of scale have yet to be realized, and the commodity is frequently produced in small lots by small producers. Products and firms that survive this first stage next enter the maturing product stage, during which increasing mechanization makes possible mass production and a dramatic increase in the industry's output. The maturing product stage witnesses the introduction of specialized machinery that reduces the ratio of labor to capital in the production process and renders the industry more capital-intensive. New production technologies, in turn, attract more resources to the industry, which soon comes to be characterized by substantial growth. The maturing product stage also witnesses the expansion of the industry into selected export markets that, in turn, become increasingly competitive. Eventually, as product specifications become standardized, and as competing regions and industries adopt or imitate comparable production technologies, the industry's original output reaches a plateau and its share of the market begins to stabilize or even contract. As the product becomes increasingly standardized in increasingly competitive markets, factor costs and combinations become critical determinants of the region's ability to retain its comparative advantage in the production of the commodity. Demand becomes far more price-sensitive as consumers become more discriminating and are presented with an expanded array of alternatives.

Individual product life cycles may be aggregated into large industrial life cycles even though any single industry may be characterized simultaneously by a complex accumulation of diverse products in various stages of development.[10] Such aggregated product cycles within a single industry can still be represented by the now familiar S-shaped curve of industrial growth that traces the evolution and migration of an industry over time (see Figure 5.1). Each phase of an industry's life cycle is accompanied by particular spatial dynamics. As an industry matures, for example, production of a particular good is likely to migrate to competing locations as they adopt or imitate the technologies that make production on a large scale feasible. Thus, the economic landscape is characterized by continuously expanding and contracting industries, and hence by concentration into and dispersion out of specific locations.

It is important to reemphasize that the life cycle hypothesis, although registered in trends at the aggregate level, can ultimately be traced back to a strong behavioral assumption at the micro level. Firms will seek to stay in or migrate from a location at which they are afforded a comparative advantage. It is this point, in fact, that distinguishes the life cycle hypothesis from other phenomena, such as biological or mechanical cycles, that demonstrate the "ebb and flow"

FIGURE 5.1
Spatial Manifestation of Product Cycle over Time

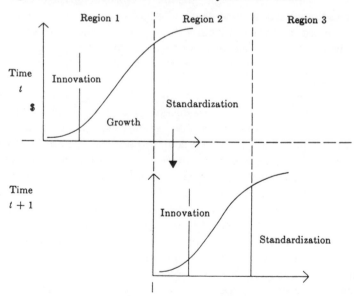

Source: John Rees, "Regional Industrial Shifts in the U.S. and the Internal Generation of Manufacturing in Growth Centers of the Southwest," in William C. Wheaton, *Interregional Movements and Regional Growth* (Washington, D.C.: Urban Institute, 1979).

characteristic. The S-curve of the life cycle is not deterministic in a biological or mechanical sense. It is the resultant of conscious calculations and choices perceived as rational by individual economic actors within the context of specific market circumstances. In other words, the birth of an industry occurs because an entrepreneur decides that a particular enterprise in a particular location at a particular time will be profitable. The industry matures if it is profitable, and greater resources are invested by the firm as demand for its product increases. At some point, should the firm decide that a continued investment of resources in that location is no longer a profitable undertaking, the industry contracts. At each phase of the cycle, therefore, the scale and location of an industrial activity is the resultant of individual choices.

The life cycle hypothesis illustrates the manner in which both the structural and spatial features of an industry are transformed over time by market choices. It offers a view of a dynamic spatial ordering of production and patterns of trade shaped by the locational decisions of individual firms as they alter their combination of factor inputs in response to changing production technologies and demand. Another point deserves considerable emphasis as well. Although the life cycle hypothesis explains the mechanics of the process of industrial change, it also imbues that process with an aura of inevitability. The most powerful lesson of the life cycle hypothesis, in fact, may be that it points to the existence of a process that is often denied: a regenerative process that operates to the advantage of an industry in the larger economy even though it may entail disadvantages for specific locations over time. This is a theme that will be developed throughout this chapter, and it is against this backdrop that the notion of industrial policy will be examined.

INDUSTRIAL POLICY AND INDUSTRIAL CHANGE

The case for industrial policy was first articulated in 1979 by Gail Schwartz and Pat Choate in their *National Sectoral Policies: A New Tool for Revitalizing the United States Economy.*[11] Warning that "the threat of disruption to American society posed by troubled industries" is a crisis that will challenge the United States for the remainder of the century, Schwartz and Choate argue that it 'is in the national interest to forge a regular, close, visible and permanent linkage between business and government."[12] Specifically, they urge the formulation of "national sectoral policies" consistent with the nation's "geo-political objectives" that include fiscal, monetary, spatial, sectoral, and regulatory interventions in the market system to direct the flow of economic resources to their most efficient, productive, and profitable uses.[13]

Schwartz and Choate were followed in 1980 by the publication of Lester Thurow's *The Zero-Sum Society.*[14] Asserting that "investment decisions have become too important to be left to the private market alone," Thurow argued that "Japan Inc. needs to be met with U.S.A. Inc."[15] Specifically, Thurow proposed the creation of "the national equivalent of a corporate investment committee to redirect investment flows from our 'sunset' industries to our 'sunrise' industries."[16] In essence, Thurow's arguments are founded on the presumption that, to the extent government helps workers and resources make the transition from declining to growth industries, the risk of industrial change is "spread" or socialized among all citizens, a presumption that is frequently used to justify public sector investments.[17]

Although Schwartz and Choate, along with Thurow, should be rightly considered the initiators of industrial policy advocacy, the mantle of leadership has passed to Robert Reich,[18] whose arguments start with the proposition that the U.S. economy is insufficiently adaptive to new challenges and a rapidly changing market place:

> America has a choice: It can adapt itself to the new economic realities by altering its organization, or it can fail to adapt and thereby continue its present decline. . . .But failure to adapt will rend the social fabric irreparably. Adaptation is America's challenge. It is America's next frontier.[19]

Specifically, Reich urges the creation of "regional development banks" along the lines of the Reconstruction Finance Corporation of the Depression era, to provide low-interest loans and subsidies that would promote the restructuring of declining industries.[20] As with Thurow's proposal, this is based on the presumption that the public sector can effectively promote industrial change through "risk-spreading." Additionally, however, Reich's proposals include the formation of an unemployment voucher system through which the federal government would subsidize the retraining of displaced workers and the training of the chronically unemployed.[21]

A broader, more explicitly spatial, response to industrial change is called for by Barry Bluestone and Bennett Harrison in *The Deindustrialization of America*.[22] Asserting that private firms, through their preoccupation with turning a profit, are recklessly "deindustrializing" the U.S. economy, Bluestone and Harrison present a case for centralized economic planning, the object being "national economic democracy."[23] Specifically, the Bluestone and Harrison proposals entail restrictions on plant closings and/or the subsidization/nationalization of certain industries.[24] Further, and perhaps more importantly, they argue that there is a need for government to play a greater role in the day-to-day operations of the individual firm; decisions concerning pricing, location, acquisition of resources, hiring and promotions, health and safety, and environmental protection are to be made by "cooperative councils" composed of representatives from industry, labor, and government. Indeed, for Bluestone and Harrison, "a rising standard of living for working people, more equally shared," rather than profit, will be the criterion upon which economic decisions are based.[25] Far more explicit than other proponents of market intervention, Bluestone and Harrison, in short, endorse the limited socialization of the U.S. economy.

The two bodies of literature examined in the chapter thus far—the life cycle model of industrial development and the several proposals for industrial policy—provide an explanation of the manner in which an industry is changed over time by market forces and a description of the character of policies that are intended to influence such change. Taken together, this discussion of industrial change and industrial policy provides a template useful for examining the evolution of a specific industry—in this case, the Texas Gulf Coast rice farming industry. The life cycle hypothesis, for example, suggests a number of benchmarks in the continuous adjustments of an industry like rice farming. Over time, these adjustments in aggregate manifest themselves in the S-shaped curve of industrial growth, maturation, and contraction. This adjustment process culminates in declining market shares for selected producers in an increasingly competitive industry attributable to rapidly rising production costs relative to productivity. These benchmarks suggest an industry that is undergoing a profound transformation. One stage of this transformation involves the drift to new factor employments at a single location; a subsequent stage involves the migration of production between locations. Together, they suggest that as an industry becomes increasingly uncompetitive it gradually substitutes one set of production arrangements for another until even location itself becomes negotiable. At that point, a now inferior spatial ordering of productive resources yields to one that is superior.

The review of industrial policies, by the same token, suggests the existence of important benchmarks as well. As was noted at the beginning of this chapter, there is a similarity between intervention in the agricultural sector and intervention in the industrial sector—a relationship that has only recently been recognized by participants in the industrial policy debate. Thurow, for instance, has argued that "in agriculture what started as a desperate effort to prop up a very large, sick industry in the 1930's ended as an industry that is the world's most efficient. There is no reason that feat cannot be duplicated elsewhere."[26] Indeed, the efficacy of industrial policies intended to promote both economic efficiency and equity may be tested by examining the application of similar policies in the argicultural sector.

POLICY RESPONSES TO STRUCTURAL CHANGE IN THE TEXAS GULF COAST RICE FARMING INDUSTRY

The rice farming industry in Texas, like most agricultural industries elsewhere in the United States, has registered the effects of substantial federal intervention over the past half-century. An examination of the Texas Gulf Coast rice farming industry, therefore, provides not only an example of the manner in which an industry is inevitably transformed by market forces over time but, more importantly, a means of evaluating policies that were intended to forestall or otherwise mitigate the effects of that transformation. This discussion will chart the evolution of the Texas Gulf Coast rice farming industry by examining the industry's long-term production trends, its changing role in the marketplace, and the recent difficulties faced by regional producers in the form of rapidly accelerating costs of production. It will, following the life cycle approach reviewed previously, demonstrate that the evolution of the industry has been marked by distinct phases, each of which is characterized by a distinctive spatial reordering of productive resources as farmers have responded to changing location-rent differentials.

The Texas Gulf Coast rice farming industry is composed of rice farming activity in eighteen Texas counties (see Figure 5.2). As of 1982, 24.1 percent of this region's total cropland was devoted to rice farming, and at the individual county level, cash receipts from rice farming were responsible for up to 22.3 percent of total personal income in 1979.[27] These data, of course, do not capture the secondary or tertiary effects of the value added from regional milling, storage, and shipping activities, or the expenditure of earned income in the regional economy.

Production Trends in the Evolution of the Industry

A clear picture of the growth and recent contraction of the Texas Gulf Coast rice farming industry may be gained by charting the industry's changing patterns of production. Indeed, a careful examination of changes in industry output reveals several distinct phases in the life of the industry that appear to correspond to the introduction of new production technologies and the stimulus of new market opportunities. Following the life cycle approach, this discussion will identify four distinct phases in the life of the Texas Gulf Coast rice farming industry: a preindustrial phase, lasting from roughly the middle to the end of the nineteenth century; a takeoff phase, lasting from approximately the beginning to the middle of the twentieth century; a maturing phase, lasting from roughly 1955 through the 1960s; and, finally, a contracting phase, which covers the past decade or so (see Figure 5.3).

The preindustrial phase: Rice cultivation on the Texas Gulf Coast began with the arrival of the first Anglo-American settlers in Texas during the middle of the nineteenth century. In these early years, Texas Gulf Coast rice farming was a primitive, infant industry not very dissimilar from rice farming in the peasant economies of monsoon Asia. Prior to the introduction of machinery, for example, rice was hand sown on low ground that would catch and hold a sufficient amount of rainwater to ensure survival. Oxen were usually employed to trample the seed into the earth. At the end of the season the farmer hand-cut the ri-

FIGURE 5.2
Location of Texas Gulf Coast Rice Farming Industry

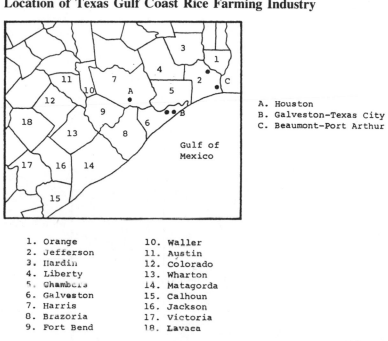

A. Houston
B. Galveston-Texas City
C. Beaumont-Port Arthur

1. Orange	10. Waller
2. Jefferson	11. Austin
3. Hardin	12. Colorado
4. Liberty	13. Wharton
5. Chambers	14. Matagorda
6. Galveston	15. Calhoun
7. Harris	16. Jackson
8. Brazoria	17. Victoria
9. Fort Bend	18. Lavaca

Source: Harold T. Gross and Andre N. Van Chau, *The Texas Gulf Coast Rice Farming Industry: Long-Term Prospects and Short-Term Alternatives* (Beaumont, Tex.: John Gray Institute, 1984).

pened grain with a scythe and tied it in bundles that were left in the field to dry. After drying, the bundles were held over a barrel while the grain was beaten off the straw. The hulls were then rubbed off the grain with a mortar and pestle to produce the consumable commodity.

Because of the primitive, labor-intensive techniques involved in the production process, the level of production, in terms of both cultivated acreage and output, remained consistently low until the beginning of the nineteenth century.[28] Indeed, it was not until 1886 that the introduction of machinery made possible the commercial cultivation of rice on a larger scale. By this time, Texas Gulf Coast farmers had begun using a walking plow pulled by oxen to prepare relatively large fields bordered by hand-dug levees that permitted irrigation from neighboring bayous and marshes. When the grain was ripe at the end of the season, it was cut by a mule-drawn binder; following a period during which it was allowed to dry, it was threshed with a steam-powered separator. The use of such machinery became so widespread that it revolutionized Texas Gulf Coast rice farming and by the end of the century sparked a boom in land sales.

FIGURE 5.3
Life Cycle of Texas Gulf Coast Rice Farming Industry

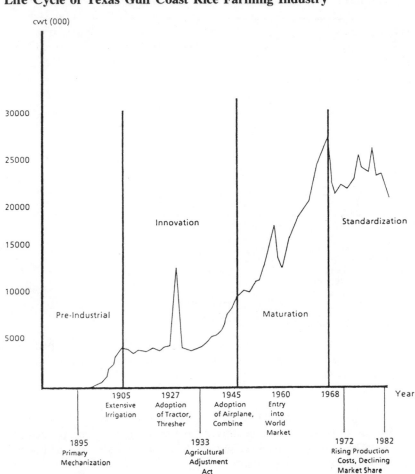

Source: Harold T. Gross and Andre N. Van Chau, *The Texas Gulf Coast Rice Farming Industry: Long-Term Prospects and Short-Term Alternatives* (Beaumont, Tex.: John Gray Institute, 1984).

The takeoff phase: The influx of new farmers along with the widespread use of machinery resulted in a dramatic transformation of Texas Gulf Coast rice farming. Cultivated acreage increased from only 5,000 acres in 1895 to 165,00 acres by 1905, while production increased from 90,000 hundredweight to 3,082,000 hundredweight during the same period.[29] The spotty cultivation of a minor cash crop had become a major agricultural industry.

From 1905 until roughly 1945, both cultivated acreage and production generally increased steadily.[30] In fact, except for two noteworthy events, the period was quite unremarkable. First, in 1920, the tractor displaced the traditional mule- or oxen-driven plow. Simultaneously, gasoline-powered threshers were introduced to replace the older steam-powered model. As the use of these new implements became widespread by the mid-1920s, substantial increases in productivity were registered.[31] Second, the early 1930s saw the beginning of substantial federal policy intervention in agriculture. For the Texas Gulf Coast rice farming industry, the immediate consequences of this intervention were twofold. First, in 1931, the U.S. Department of Agriculture inaugurated a large cooperative rice research and breeding program in cooperation with the Texas Agricultural Extension Service. This marked the beginning of a program of research that would spawn useful technological innovations in later years. Second, in 1933, Texas Gulf Coast rice farmers, along with other U.S. farmers, became eligible for the Department of Agriculture's package of acreage diversion and price support programs offered in the Agricultural Adjustment Act of 1933.

The mature-industry phase: The early postwar years saw the introduction of a number of technological innovations that were largely responsible for rapid increases posted in both cultivated acreage and production during the 1945–54 period. For example, in 1945, the airplane was introduced to Texas Gulf Coast rice farming, and within three years almost all of the rice cultivated on the Texas Gulf Coast was air-seeded into flooded fields. Too, by the late 1940s, most Texas Gulf Coast producers had discarded the now-obsolete tractor-pulled threshers in favor of self-propelled combines. Finally, farmers were also starting to benefit from technological innovations introduced by the Texas Agricultural Extension Service. Thus, the 1945–54 period was generally one of very rapid growth for the industry.

The ultimate effect of these innovations, however, was to allow the United States—and the Texas Gulf Coast—to become an important participant in the world market for rice. During the first half of the twentieth century, for instance, the United States, though a substantial exporter, was of only secondary importance in the world market, well behind such traditional exporters as British India, Burma, Thailand, and French Indochina. Since the end of World War II, however, major changes in rice trading patterns have taken place. India, since the end of British rule, has all but abandoned the market, emerging only infrequently to barter rice with the Soviet Union and Vietnam. Burma, experimenting with political and economic isolation, allowed its rice exports to plunge abruptly below 1 million metric tons in 1966, where they have since remained. Vietnam has been importing large quantities of rice for the past two decades and will likely continue to do so for the foreseeable future. Of the four traditional large exporters, only Thailand has retained a significant share of the world market. Propelled by technological innovations that made possible large increases in production, the United States—and particularly the Texas Gulf Coast—moved into the void created by the withdrawal of three traditional large exporters and became a major supplier to the world market.[32]

The sequence of events characterizing the three phases described above—

preindustrial, takeoff, and mature-industry—conforms closely to the scenario described by the life cycle model. A primitive, labor-intensive production technology that inhibits industry growth and output is gradually replaced by an increasing level of mechanization that makes growth and increased output feasible. The increasing capital intensity of the industry allows it to achieve economies of scale in production that, in turn, allow it to capture large export markets. But the expansion that characterizes these phases in the life of the industry is also a precursor to the stability and contraction that must inevitably follow. As the product becomes standardized, and as competing regions adopt or imitate comparable production technologies, competition in markets at several scales increases, and the costs of factor inputs emerge as more critical determinants of the ability of an industry anchored to a specific location to sustain its comparative advantage.

Evidence of contraction: During the past decade, and in sharp contrast to the rapid growth of the past thirty years, the Texas Gulf Coast rice farming industry has been characterized by essentially stagnant levels of cultivated acreage and production. From 1972 to 1982, the total number of acres of cropland on the Texas Gulf Coast devoted to rice farming increased by less than 1 percent (see Table 5.1). However, this aggregate value masks a pattern of changes at the individual county level through which the industry may be seen to have retreated to only eleven of the original eighteen counties in which rice has traditionally been grown. Similarly, production increased only marginally over the 1972–82 period and, as with acreage, contracted to fewer counties along the Texas Gulf Coast.

In order to gain a greater appreciation of the significance of the recent stagnation in cultivated acreage and production, it is important to consider the industry's changing role in the marketplace. Such an examination is useful, not only because it provides additional evidence of an industry gradually being decoupled from a regional economy, but also because it implicitly suggests the cause of such change: rising opportunity costs that initiate a gradual migration of production to alternative locations. As recently as the early 1970s, the Texas Gulf Coast rice farming industry was the leading supplier to the domestic market and was consistently at or near the top of the international market. In the past decade, however, the locational consequences of domestic competition and resource constraints besetting rice production in this region have become unmistakably clear.

Although the domestic demand for rice has increased substantially over the past decade, the Texas Gulf Coast rice farming industry appears to be in a state of fairly steady contraction. In 1972, for instance, the rice produced by the Texas Gulf Coast accounted for 25.8 percent of the nation's total output of rice. Yet, by 1982, that proportion had fallen to only 14.3 percent.[33] Indeed, although the Texas Gulf Coast was the nation's leading producer of rice in 1972, by 1982 Texas ranked fourth behind Arkansas, California, and Louisiana (see Table 5.2). While rice production on the Texas Gulf Coast stagnated from 1972 to 1982, competing domestic growers boosted their production by at least 24 percent.

TABLE 5.1
Change in Texas Gulf Coast Rice Agriculture by County, 1972–82

	Acreage				Production		
County	1982	1972	Percent Change 1972–82	County	1982	1972	Percent Change 1972–82
Calhoun	12,400	6,200	97.5	Calhoun	620,000 cwt.	307,000 cwt.	102.0
Galveston	8,600	4,710	82.6	Hardin	72,000	42,000	71.4
Hardin	1,600	1,110	44.1	Victoria	289,000	201,000	43.8
Victoria	5,400	3,920	37.8	Galveston	250,000	197,000	26.9
Colorado	45,000	37,800	19.1	Colorado	2,348,000	1,997,000	17.6
Wharton	80,000	70,200	14.0	Wharton	4,188,000	3,637,000	15.2
Jackson	36,800	33,400	10.2	Austin	205,000	181,000	13.3
Brazoria	49,000	45,600	7.5	Matagorda	2,432,000	2,309,000	5.3
Matagorda	48,500	46,800	3.6	Fort Bend	1,017,000	968,000	5.1
Austin	4,000	3,870	3.4	Waller	749,000	729,000	2.7
Chambers	44,000	42,600	3.3	Brazoria	1,960,000	1,910,000	2.6
Fort Bend	21,500	22,100	−2.7	Jackson	1,702,000	1,665,000	2.2
Liberty	34,100	36,900	−7.6	Chambers	1,854,000	1,911,000	−3.0
Waller	13,500	15,200	−11.2	Liberty	1,542,000	1,691,000	−8.8
Lavaca	4,800	6,260	−23.3	Lavaca	217,000	300,000	−29.1
Jefferson	43,000	61,200	−29.7	Harris	920,000	1,365,000	−32.6
Harris	18,000	24,264	−34.8	Jefferson	1,680,000	2,564,000	−34.5
Orange	1,500	2,440	−38.5	Orange	44,000	97,000	−54.6
Texas Gulf Coast	471,700	469,000	0.6	Texas Gulf Coast	22,089,000	22,077,000	0.1

Source: Texas Department of Agriculture, *1972 and 1982 Texas Field Crop Statistics* (Austin: Texas Department of Agriculture).

TABLE 5.2
U.S. Rice Production Ranked by Region, 1972 and 1982

1972 Ranking		1982 Ranking	
Region	Production	Region	Production
Texas Gulf Coast	22,077,000 cwt.	Arkansas	57,037,000 cwt.
Arkansas	21,939,000	California	36,651,000
Louisiana	19,967,000	Louisiana	24,862,000
California	18,868,000	Texas Gulf Coast	22,089,000
Mississippi	2,325,000	Mississippi	9,870,000
Missouri	218,000	Missouri	3,582,000

Source: U.S. Department of Agriculture, *1974 Agriculture Statistics* (Washington, D.C.: U.S. G.P.O., 1975); Texas Department of Agriculture, *1982 Texas Field Crop Statistics* (Austin: Texas Department of Agriculture, 1983).

Similar circumstances prevail with regard to the international marketplace. In 1972, commercial export of rice from the Texas Gulf Coast accounted for 8 percent of the world's total commercial exports. By 1982, that proportion had fallen to 7 percent despite a rapidly increasing world demand for rice.[34] More to the point is the fact that the Texas Gulf Coast appears to be losing its position among the world's leading exporters of rice. In 1972, the Texas Gulf Coast was the world's fourth largest exporter of rice, behind Thailand, a conglomerate of competing domestic producers, and China (see Table 5.3). By 1980, however, the Texas Gulf Coast had fallen to fifth, having been passed by Pakistan; even that position now appears threatened given the rapid increases in exports posted by Japan. Thus, in the international market, the Texas Gulf Coast rice farming industry appears unable to keep pace with its competitors despite the new opportunities created by a rapidly growing market.

Both of these phenomena suggest that the terms of trade have changed; that is, the opportunity costs associated with rice production on the Texas Gulf Coast are increasing. Indeed, the recent stagnation of production and loss of market share experienced by the industry suggest that the costs of factor inputs to rice production not only vary spatially but, in the case of the Texas Gulf Coast, are actually outpacing productivity. The rather strong behavioral assumption of the life cycle hypothesis, in turn, suggests that increasing opportunity costs—manifested in rapidly increasing factor input costs—will encourage producers to seek alternative uses for their resources. An examination of the Texas Gulf Coast growers' production costs using financial data obtained from the region's agricultural lenders, in fact, suggests that this is indeed the case. Over the past decade, the costs per acre of three critical factor inputs—water, chemicals, and capital equipment—have increased by over 100 percent, although over the same period, productivity remained unchanged.[35] Moreover, the increases in produc-

TABLE 5.3
Rice Exporters by Rank, 1972 and 1980

Exporter	1972 Exports	Exporter	1980 Exports
Thailand	2,076,000 mt.	Thailand	2,700,000 mt.
United States[a]	1,364,310	United States[a]	2,114,404
China	815,000	China	1,000,000
Texas Gulf Coast	600,849	Pakistan	968,000
Burma	511,000	Texas Gulf Coast	893,536
Pakistan	300,540	Burma	675,000
Japan	182,666	Japan	653,000

[a]Excluding Texas Gulf Coast.

Source: U.S. Department of Agriculture, *1974 and 1982 Agricultural Statistics* (Washington, D.C.: U.S. G.P.O., 1975 and 1983); Texas Department of Agriculture, *1972 and 1980 Texas Field Crop Statistics* (Austin: Texas Department of Agriculture, 1973 and 1981).

tion registered by competing regions have tended to force market prices for the commodity downward so that the Texas Gulf Coast producer is caught in an increasingly untenable position.[36]

As with the earlier phases, the sequence of events described in this phase conforms to the scenario outlined in the life cycle model. Rapidly rising factor input costs against a stagnant level of productivity resulting, in turn, in a diminished market share for the industry provide a graphic illustration of the dynamics underlying the industry's contraction. Indeed, rising factor input costs are evidence of shifting location-rent differentials to which Texas Gulf Coast rice producers are responding by withdrawing land from cultivation.

Policy Intervention in the Rice Farming Industry

As was noted previously, the Texas Gulf Coast rice farming industry has experienced substantial federal policy intervention over the past half-century; from this experience, a number of implications for policy intervention in goods- and service-producing sectors can be derived. Intervention in the agricultural sector has traditionally taken the form of federal price support programs and applied research efforts by federal and state agricultural services. Have these two forms of policy intervention promoted efficiency in the Texas Gulf Coast rice farming industry as it progressed through the phases of its life cycle?

The principal goals of federal price support programs are not and never have been intended to promote efficiency, despite Thurow's implication to the contrary. Indeed, the primary objectives of federal price support and associated cropland diversion programs have been considerably more limited. The achievement of commodity price stability and increased farm incomes have been the overriding goals. Although specific programs tend to vary somewhat in the short run, the legislation introduced in the Agricultural Adjustment Act of 1933 continues to serve as a basic framework for federal intervention in the agricultural sector. Indeed, the most important objectives of agricultural intervention have remained essentially unchanged over the past half-century. They are:

1. To raise the average level of farm incomes to a satisfactory level through stability in farm prices without imposing unacceptably high costs upon taxpayers;
2. To improve the competitiveness of U.S. agricultural products in export markets while protecting markets from imports of competitive products;
3. To insure an adequate supply of agricultural products to U.S. consumers at acceptable prices.[37]

Efficiency has been considered a desirable, though indirect, outcome thought to be attainable as farmers withhold marginal croplands from production in order to qualify for federal price supports. Accordingly, if an examination of federal price support programs is restricted to asking whether or not they have successfully achieved their primary objectives, the answer is generally yes. To the extent price support and acreage diversion programs effectively restrict the supply of farm commodities to consumers and simultaneously transfer income to the farm community, both farm prices and incomes have been substantially higher than they would have been in the absence of such intervention.[38] Indeed, in the absence of the considerable subsidies received by Texas Gulf Coast producers, there can be little doubt that the industry would be considerably smaller than it is today and would have moved more rapidly into successive phases of its life cycle. Even these successes, however, are quite limited if viewed within the context of the industry's evolution over time. Despite having benefited from acreage diversion and price support programs since the early 1930s, the Texas Gulf Coast rice farming industry has nonetheless evolved through the phases of its life cycle. As a result, federal price support programs should properly be viewed as essentially a short-term expedient. They may serve, in other words, to mitigate the effects accompanying structural change, but they do not—indeed cannot—arrest or impede the process of industrial change itself. To the extent that such programs have effectively insulated Texas Gulf Coast producers from adjustments to changes in the terms of trade, they have also distorted the price signals that would have directed the farmer's use of productive resources over the long term into more sustainable activities such as animal husbandry and aquaculture.

A second form of intervention believed to offer the promise of regaining lost comparative advantage or creating comparative advantage anew involves the applied research programs that have received considerable attention in the agricultural sector. Unlike federal price support programs that do not include efficiency as a stated objective, the primary goal of federally and state-funded agricultural research programs has been to improve the productivity of U.S. farms. Have research and technological innovation promoted increased productivity and, hence, an efficient employment of resources in the agricultural sector? A number of studies argue that applied research has indeed achieved this objective.[39] But to examine the efficacy of applied research as a promoter of efficiency solely on the basis of the rate of return on financial resources invested in research, however, is to ignore more important temporal and spatial questions. As was pointed out earlier, technological innovations that were the outcome of applied research efforts made possible the growth of the Texas Gulf Coast rice farming industry in response to opportunities created by the withdrawal of several traditional rice exporters from the world market during the 1950s. As with federal price support programs however, subsequent research failed to arrest or impede the movement of the industry through the phases of its life cycle. That R & D or applied research can dampen or reverse the downward trend in an industry's S-curve during the maturation and standardized product phases of its life cycle by providing the impetus to new growth cycles appears to be a misconception. Indeed, such a notion implicitly presumes that innovation and, more importantly, diffusion throughout the original producing region outpaces the adoption of similar innovations in competing regions. This perspective ignores the inherently spatial nature of technological innovation, a topic developed in Chapter 3. With regard to rice farming, for example, the steadily declining traded ratio of rice in the countries of monsoon Asia is principally a consequence of the adoption of technological innovations such as high-yield varieties and extensive irrigation by producers in those countries over the past decade (see Table 5.4). Moreover, while research does make a substantial, indeed necessary, contribution to efficiency and output during the innovation phase, and perhaps even well into the maturation phase, it becomes increasingly unimportant as competing regions quickly adopt innovations and eventually become seedbeds of innovation themselves. The increasing self-sufficiency of traditional rice importing nations, for instance, strongly suggests that research in the United States is matched by or may even be inferior to the research performed at rice research centers in competing regions.[40] And as with price support programs, the promise of applied research has probably encouraged farmers to resist the changes that are being foisted upon them by the dynamics of the marketplace in the mistaken hope that research will resolve their problems.

What, then, has intervention in the Texas Gulf Coast rice farming industry, in the form of either price support programs or applied research efforts, achieved? In a limited sense, intervention in both forms has served to dull successfully the effects of structural change, insulating many Texas Gulf Coast rice farmers from adjustment to the new realities of a changing marketplace. In the absence of intervention, Texas Gulf Coast rice farmers would, at the micro level,

TABLE 5.4
Percentage of Ricelands in Monsoon Asia Sown with High-Yield Varieties, Irrigated, or Shallow Rainfed

Country	Ricelands Irrigated	Ricelands Irrigated or Shallow Rainfed	Ricelands Sown with High-Yield Varieties
Bangladesh	11.0	33.0	15.0
Burma	16.0	96.0	6.0
China	90.0	98.0	N.A.
India	39.0	72.0	28.0
Indonesia	39.0	59.0	40.0
Japan	96.0	96.0	N.A.
Korea	92.0	100.0	26.0
Malaysia	63.0	88.0	38.0
Nepal	17.0	92.0	18.0
Pakistan	100.0	100.0	39.0
Sri Lanka	50.0	83.0	67.0
Thailand	24.0	49.0	7.0
Vietnam	13.0	70.0	30.0

Sources: Randolph Barker and R.W. Herdt, *Rainfed Lowland Rice as a Research Priority—An Economist's View,* Research Paper No. 26 (Los Banos: International Rice Research Institute, 1979) and Adelita C. Palacpac, *World Rice Statistics* (Los Banos, Republic of the Philippines: International Rice Research Institute, 1978).

face shifting location-rent differentials. As the discussion of factor input costs implied, the opportunity costs of employing productive resources in the cultivation of rice are increasing—a trend that *should* induce farmers to search for alternative uses for their resources. This, in turn, would be reflected in a dramatic spatial reordering of land uses as rice farmlands tied to a maturing technology would be abandoned or be allocated to other uses. At the macro level, this would be reflected in a gradual displacement of the rice industry altogether—the logical and ultimate conclusion for an industry that has passed through a succession of life stages.

To a large extent, this scenario has been realized. Changing location-rent differentials are indeed forcing some rice producers out of the industry. There has occurred some spatial reordering of the industry that is reflected in the gradual contraction of rice farming to fewer counties along the Texas Gulf Coast. This, in turn, has been accompanied by the industry's relative decline in production and loss of market share to domestic and international competitors. But the pace of the transformation experienced by the industry has been constrained by intervention. This limited impact suggests two important points. First, the fact that a considerable reallocation of productive resources formerly employed in the rice industry has taken place despite explicit policy intervention confirms both the inevitability of long-term industrial adjustment and the relative inefficiency of intervention. Second, the fact that the process of industrial change has tended to proceed despite explicit intervention directs attention to the existence of an information problem. Intervention in the Texas Gulf Coast rice farming industry has served primarily to distort the location-rent differentials that guide the farmer's resource allocation decisions. The subsidies received by farmers enrolled in federal price support programs have exerted considerable influence on the structure of the rice farming industry. Therefore, intervention has, at least for the short term, hampered the adjustment of the industry to changing markets by inducing farmers to remain tied both to traditional land uses and to inefficient production technologies long after it would have become unprofitable for them to do so in the absence of such explicit intervention. In other words, an efficient employment of economic resources cannot, by definition, be maximized in an environment in which opportunity costs are distorted by intervention; in the end, nonmarket resource allocations do not realistically reflect the comparative advantages or disadvantages associated with alternative activities and locations.

Implications for industrial sectors: Although the mechanisms for intervention in the industrial and agricultural sectors differ in detail, conceptually and effectively they are virtually identical. The resurrection of a Reconstruction Finance Corporation, as suggested by Thurow and Reich, that would offer financing to selected industries or the enactment of legislation that would prohibit or delay plant closings and provide subsidies to declining industries, as suggested by Bluestone and Harrison, are effectively the same as federal price support programs. Both industrial and agricultural adjustment policies have the effect of redistributing income from taxpayers to some industry—and, by extension, location-specific groups of recipients who are, by some criteria, deemed worthy. Both types of policies seek to allocate productive resources in a manner different than they would be directed by the market. Similarly, R&D and applied research programs that are called for in many of the proposals for industrial policy seek to stimulate or prolong an industry or region that is evidently long past its prime and characterized by an inability to remain competitive or provide the impetus to the birth and growth of new industries. As in the case of agriculture, in fact, both the process and effect of R&D and technological innovation in the industrial sector are spatially dynamic and cannot be expected to alter significantly the life cycle of an industry.[41]

To the extent that industrial policy mechanisms (broadly defined) are largely similar to those that have long been employed in the agricultural sector, there is no logical reason to expect a different outcome. Given past experience, there is every reason to expect a similar outcome, particularly when that outcome is touted as a compelling precedent to be followed. If the experiences of the agricultural sector are, as Thurow has suggested, a measure of what intervention may achieve in the industrial sector, some other criterion than economic efficiency must be employed to justify industrial policy because efficiency is the opposite of what is likely to be achieved. In agriculture generally, and as we have seen in the Texas Gulf Coast rice farming industry in particular, industrial policies are likely to produce an outcome that, in the long run, will tend toward economic inefficiency. The most likely outcome, in fact, is the creation of a set of incentives for an industry or selected group of industries that induces an inefficient employment of productive resources that can only be justified on some other grounds than efficiency. For precisely that reason, the equity criterion, which holds that new policies, programs, and institutions may be needed to secure a more equitable allocation of resources, is often invoked in its stead. The substitution of one criterion for another, however, raises as many questions as it answers, for an outcome that is considered equitable generally entails the redistribution of advantage from one group to another and the alliance of the favored group with government to the potential detriment of others.

What policy implications does this suggest? It suggests that industrial policies cannot be entirely justified by the criterion of equity when the interests of all producers and consumers are considered. It further suggests that equity may be a negotiable criterion with little inherent meaning that justifies the insulation of a politically favored industry or region from the long-term adjustment process, thereby sacrificing any long-term benefits that would otherwise accrue to the whole. This, in turn, poses an interesting question. By what criteria is an industry or region selected as the beneficiary of industrial policy?

In answering that question, policy makers must consciously choose between the preservation of existing social and political relationships and the creation of new and historically unfamiliar ones. In this context, the industrial policy debate becomes an arena for the airing of arguments shaped by traditional perceptions of problems and possible solutions. Established interests effectively focus the debate and new constituencies are not allowed to develop. The policies that emerge from this arena no longer resemble the lofty arguments that motivated them. They have given way to the political bargaining that must prevail in the struggle between competing constituencies.

A POLICY ALTERNATIVE: THE GRASSROOTS APPROACH

Rather than implementing costly new programs or modifiying existing ones that are not attuned to industrial change and that will inevitably be compromised by political bargaining, would it not be far better to allow such adjustments to proceed and naturally encourage the birth and robust health of new patterns of production, distribution, and consumption? Or, as August Losch so eloquently argued:

As soon as the breaking up of old combinations is economically justified, every attempt to obstruct it means a sacrifice. A sacrifice, however, that may be vindicated now and then by the fact that it helps to preserve the political and cultural existence of an economic landscape for a while even though it has passed its economic prime. Those who have to bear the burden in this case are the inhabitants, who, prevented from leaving, are forced to put up with a lower standard of living. In the long run they are also politically endangered thereby. If it is a case merely of a depressed area within a country, the prosperous areas generally bear the cost. This is not always a wise policy, even when the importance of extra-economic causes is freely admitted. It would often be much better to facilitate the breaking up of an old combination of land, people and economic activities and seek systematically for a new and vital one; that is, to promote adaptation rather than to obstruct it.[42]

If the objective of policy makers is indeed to nurture an efficient economy and an equitable distribution of productive resources, it is far more likely to be achieved by allowing industrial adjustments rooted in the aspirations and actions of individual producers and consumers to proceed. While this inevitably involves the gradual abandonment and eventual destruction of obsolete structures and spatial orderings of people and their property, new and vital arrangements emerge in their place.

To the extent the industrial policy debate really reflects an overwhelming concern with adaptation to the new realities of the competitive marketplace, why not start from the bottom up instead of the top down? Why not consider a grassroots approach to industrial change that emphasizes individual choice and the pursuit of new opportunities instead of the resolution of problems? Grounded in a view of the economy as a dynamic system characterized by the breakup of established patterns of production and trade and the exploitation of new opportunities, the grassroots approach calls for a highly decentralized response to industrial change based on cooperative efforts by business, labor, industry, and education at the local or regional level. The overarching purpose of such an approach should be to foster an economic climate that encourages innovation and adaptation in response to an everchanging and increasingly competitive environment. Regions and localities should specialize in the production of commodities in which they have relative cost advantages and exchange them in the marketplace for products in which they have relative cost disadvantages. Recognizing that the terms of trade may have shifted and, indeed, will continue to do so, each community must reassess its comparative strengths and weaknesses and pursue industrial and human resource development strategies that conform to these new realities.

Specifically, the grassroots approach would address three areas of importance to the long-term economic well-being of communities. First, efforts should be undertaken at the local level to promote greater economic diversification so that the community will be less vulnerable to the vicissitudes of the business cycle. Universities, for example, can assist local businesses and chambers of commerce in identifying opportunities for new and expanded ventures. Objective analyses that pinpoint an area's comparative strengths and weaknesses in terms of geography, transportation, infrastructure, and human resources, as well as profiles of the area's existing industrial structure and backward and forward linkages, are a necessary prerequisite to systematic industrial recruitment or the promotion of indigenous growth. Many cities in the Sunbelt that have been successful in expanding and diversifying their economies—Dallas, San Antonio, Phoenix, and Research Triangle Park, N.C., to name a few—have invested a great deal of time and effort in establishing solid working relationships with their local universities. University business and economics faculties should consider adopting the "extension service" concept of their cousins in the fields of agronomics and agricultural economics and provide small businesses with technical and managerial expertise and continuing education. All too often the indigenous growth of small businesses is inhibited not by a lack of ideas, but by an ignorance of the mechanics of business management. Universities can also encourage small business development and entrepreneurship by bringing together potential entrepreneurs and venture capitalists.

Second, both labor and management should work closely to reduce unnecessary, and ultimately harmful, conflict that adds to the turmoil already caused by structural change. Again, the academic community can make a positive contribution by heightening the public's awareness of labor-management issues and by providing a forum where all sides may be heard in an atmosphere of fairness and restraint. This is, perhaps, the most important component of the grassroots approach since the industries most affected by industrial change have tended to be older manufacturing industries in the Northeast and Midwest characterized by a fairly high degree of unionization. The contraction of these industries over the past few years has been accompanied by a string of wage and work-rule concessions unparalleled in the modern history of labor-management relations. As a result of two years of concession bargaining in steel, autos, rubber, and other major industries, the 1983 average contract wage settlement worked out to a mere 1.7 percent, far below the increases recorded in the late 1970s.

Finally, the grassroots approach to structural adjustment must address the critical issue of human resource development. Industrial change invariably displaces workers and alters the long-term employment prospects for a given region. Therefore, business, labor, industry, and education must work diligently to train and retrain workers for tomorrow's jobs. Labor unions must expand and broaden apprentice programs that focus on providing industrial workers with generic skills that can be transferred to new tasks. Business and industry must increase their investment in human capital through on-the-job training and advanced job-skills programs. Universities can contribute to the adjustment process through continuing education programs that emphasize vocational skills and rehabilitation and by sponsoring seminars for shop stewards, foremen, and managers to improve in-plant communication and supervision. Moreover, business and education should work together to revise professional curricula in business, economics, and engineering programs to better reflect the changing needs of the labor market.

All of these measures are directed at improving an area's business climate. Because they rely on voluntary initiatives by business, labor, industry, and education, they are far more realistic and therefore more desirable than the worn-out policies and programs currently in fashion. First and foremost, the grass-roots approach explicitly recognizes a characteristic of industrial change that industrial policy proponents often choose to ignore—that basic economic activity in a particular location cannot be forced. Or, as Alfred Marshall once so eloquently pointed out, the spirit of enterprise is something in the air of a place, and that air may go stale.

SUMMARY

The purpose of this chapter has been to examine the issue of industrial policy within a regional context by placing it in both a conceptual and an empirical perspective. Conceptually, the issue ultimately becomes one of whether or not an industrial policy should be employed to preserve existing structures that have become redundant and obsolete, or whether obsolete structures should be allowed to disappear altogether. Such a choice inevitably involves a concern for the spatial ordering of economic activity, and the issue then becomes whether or not the vitality of particular locations is to be maintained.

To a large degree, the notion that an industrial policy can halt the process of industrial change or substantially mitigate its effects is a logical consequence of the neoclassical paradigm that has dominated U.S. political economy for the past four decades. But if the paradigm of the economy as a closed system in equilibrium is replaced with a view of the economy as an open system in dynamic disequilibrium—characterized, for example, by Schumpeter's "creative destruction" and Vernon's life cycle hypothesis—the urgency, indeed relevancy, of industrial policy vanishes. Moreover, the futility of such a policy can be seen in an agricultural sector that has registered the effects of substantial federal policy intervention over the past half-century.

A viable alternative to industrial policy is a grassroots approach that is premised on the notion that structural economic change is a healthy, regenerative process that is best encouraged (or at least less constrained) by private markets. Such an approach is probably a more realistic and politically feasible response given growing regionalism and the trend toward more decentralized government in the United States.

NOTES

1. Fredrich A. Hayek, *The Constitution of Liberty* (Chicago: University of Chicago Press, 1969), 361.

2. Joseph A. Schumpeter, *Capitalism, Socialism and Democracy* (New York: Harper and Brothers, 1942).

3. Raymond Vernon, "International Investment and International Trade in the Product Cycle," *Quarterly Journal of Economics* 46 (May 1966): 113–119.

4. Seev Hirsch, *Location of Industry and International Competitiveness* (Oxford: Oxford University Press, 1967).

5. John Rees, "Decision Making, The Growth of the Firm and the Business Environment," in F.E.I. Hamilton, ed., *Spatial Perspectives on Industrial Organization and Decision Making* (London: Wiley, 1974).

6. See, for example, John Maynard Keynes, *The General Theory of Employment, Interest, and Money* (London: MacMillan, 1936).

7. Schumpeter, *Capitalism, Socialism and Democracy*, 82–83.

8. See, for example, William Alonso, *Location and Land Use: Toward a General Theory of Land Rent* (Cambridge, Mass.: Harvard University Press, 1964).

9. Johann von Thunen, *Der isolierte Staat in Beziehung auf Landwirtschaft und National-ökonomie* (Rostock, 1826); see also Peter Hall, ed., *Von Thunen's Isolated State*, trans. Carla M. Wartenberg (London: Pergamon Press, 1966).

10. John Rees, "Regional Industrial Shifts in the U.S. and the Internal Generation of Manufacturing in Growth Centers of the Southwest," in William C. Wheaton, ed., *Interregional Movements and Regional Growth* (Washington, D.C.: Urban Institute, 1979).

11. Gail Garfield Schwartz and Pat Choate, *National Sectoral Policies: A New Tool for Revitalizing the United States Economy* (Washington, D.C.: Academy for Contemporary Problems, 1979).

12. Schwartz and Choate, *National Sectoral Policies*, ii.

13. Schwartz and Choate, *National Sectoral Policies*.

14. Lester Thurow, *The Zero-Sum Society: Distribution and the Possibilities for Economic Change* (New York: Basic Books, 1980).

15. Thurow, *The Zero-Sum Society*, 192.

16. Thurow, *The Zero-Sum Society*, 95.

17. See, for example, Kenneth J. Arrow and R.C. Lind, "Uncertainty and the Evaluation of Public Investment Decisions," *American Economic Review* 60 (June 1970): 364–378.

18. Robert Reich, *The Next American Frontier* (New York: Times Books, 1983).

19. Reich, *The Next American Frontier*, 21.

20. Reich, *The Next American Frontier*, 8.

21. Reich, *The Next American Frontier*, 248.

22. Barry Bluestone and Bennett Harrison, *The Deindustrialization of America: Plant Closings, Community Abandonment, and the Dismantling of Basic Industries* (New York: Basic Books, 1982).

23. Bluestone and Harrison, *Deindustrialization of America*, 244–245.

24. Bluestone and Harrison, *Deindustrialization of America*, 244–245.

25. Bluestone and Harrison, *Deindustrialization of America*, 256. The reader may also wish to consult the following: Amitai Etzioni, *An Immodest Agenda: Rebuilding America Before the Twenty-First Century* (New York: McGraw-Hill, 1983); Ira C. Magaziner and Robert Reich, *Minding America's Business* (Englewood Cliffs, N.J.: Prentice-Hall, 1982); and Lester Thurow, "America in a Competitive Economic World," in G.W. Miller, ed., *Regrowing the American Economy* (Englewood Cliffs, N.J.: Prentice-Hall, 1983).

26. Lester Thurow, "Farms: A Policy Success," *Newsweek*, May 16, 1983, p. 19.

27. Harold T. Gross and Andre N. Van Chau, *The Texas Gulf Coast Rice Farming Industry:*

Long-Term Prospects and Short Term Alternatives (Beaumont, Tex.: John Gray Institute, 1984), 3–6.

28. Gross and Van Chau, *Texas Gulf Coast Rice Farming Industry,* 9, 10.

29. Gross and Van Chau, *Texas Gulf Coast Rice Farming Industry,* 11.

30. Gross and Van Chau, *Texas Gulf Coast Rice Farming Industry,* 11.

31. Gross and Van Chau, *Texas Gulf Coast Rice Farming Industry,* 11.

32. Gross and Van Chau, *Texas Gulf Coast Rice Farming Industry,* 41–42.

33. Gross and Van Chau, *Texas Gulf Coast Rice Farming Industry,* 29.

34. Gross and Van Chau, *Texas Gulf Coast Rice Farming Industry,* 51.

35. Gross and Van Chau, *Texas Gulf Coast Rice Farming Industry,* 58.

36. Gross and Van Chau, *Texas Gulf Coast Rice Farming Industry,* 61–64.

37. Luther Tweeten, "Objectives of U.S. Food and Agricultural Policy and Implications for Commodity Legislation," in *Farm and Food Policy 1977* (Washington, D.C.: U.S. Senate, Committee on Agriculture and Forestry, 94th Congress, 2nd Session, 1976).

38. See, for example, A. Barry Carr and Luther Tweeten, *Comparative Efficiency of Selected Voluntary Acreage Control Programs in the Use of Government Funds,* Oklahoma Agricultural Experiment Station Research Report No. P–696 (Stillwater: Oklahoma State University, 1974); R.P. Christensen and R.O. Aines, *Economic Effects of Acreage Control Programs in the 1950's,* Agricultural Economic Report No. 18 (Washington, D.C.: U.S. Department of Agriculture, Economic Research Service, 1962); Rachel Dardis and Janet Dennisson, "The Welfare Cost of Alternative Methods for Protecting Raw Wool in the United States," *American Journal of Agricultural Economics* 51 (1969): 303–319; L.F. Husliak, "A Welfare Analysis of the Voluntary Corn Diversion Program, 1961–1966," *American Journal of Agricultural Economics* 53 (1971): 173–181; P.R. Johnson, "The Social Costs of the Tobacco Program," *Journal of Farm Economics* 46 (1965): 242–255; Frederick Nelson and Willard Cochrane, "Economic Consequences of Federal Farm Commodity Programs, 1953–1972, "*Agricultural Economics Research* 28 (1976): 52–64; Leroy Quance and Luther Tweeten, "Excess Capacity and Adjustment Potential in U.S. Agriculture," *Agricultural Economics Research* 24 (1972): 57–66; Fred Tyner and Luther Tweeten, "Express Capacity in U.S. Agriculture," *Agricultural Economics Research* 16 (1964): 23–31; Tyner and Tweeten, "Optimum Resource Allocation in U.S. Agriculture," *American Journal of Agricultural Economics* 48 (1966): 613–631; and Tyner and Tweeten, "Simulation as a Method of Appraising Farm Programs," *American Journal of Agricultural Economics* 44 (1962): 580–594.

39. See, for example, Fred C. White and Joseph Havlicek, Jr., "Optimal Expenditures for Agricultural Research and Extension: Implications of Underfunding," *American Journal of Agricultural Economics* 64 (February 1982): 47–55; and Phillip L. Cline and Yao-Chi Lu, "Efficiency Aspects of the Spatial Allocation of Public Sector Agricultural Research and Extension in the United States," *Regional Science Perspectives* 6 (1976): 1–16.

40. Gross and Van Chau, *Texas Gulf Coast Rice Farming Industry,* 71.

41. See Rees, "Regional Industrial Shifts in the U.S."

42. August Losch, *The Economics of Location,* trans. William H. Woglom (New Haven, Conn.: Yale University Press, 1956) 326–327.

6

Emerging
Regional Issues

The previous chapters have discussed in detail both the causes and consequences of interregional migration and differential economic growth in the United States. In concluding this study, we shall attempt to relate our findings to a number of important policy issues, at both national and regional levels, that have evolved in recent years as a result of shifting regional economic circumstances. Does the United States need a regional or balanced national growth policy? In a similar vein, does the United States need a comprehensive "national industrial policy"? More generally, is a redirection of federal spending an appropriate response to the phenomenon of lagging regions and industries? What are the state and local public sector implications of regional growth and decline?

THE NATIONAL PERSPECTIVE

At present, the United States has no national policies dealing with population growth, population distribution, balanced economic development, or industrial change. While a wide variety of federal programs, from military procurement to "bail-outs" of troubled industries, have undoubtedly had differential regional impacts, these programs are not specifically intended to influence the regional distribution of economic activity. The recent growth of the Sunbelt, coupled with economic stagnation prevalent in parts of the North, has led some observers to suggest that balanced regional economic development or the development of specific industries should be incorporated as a major objective of federal economic policies and actions. Such an approach, however, would be counterproductive.

Note: Some of the material in this chapter appeared originally in the July/August 1982 issue of *Society* (Vol. 19, No. 5) and is reproduced with permission.

At issue here is whether or not the dynamics of the marketplace are creating an optimal spatial arrangement of economic activity over time. It must be remembered, however, that the United States is an open economy with different and continuously changing regional endowments and specializations. Thus, we should not be surprised to observe differential economic growth rates as technology, aggregate demand, and factor endowments change over time. Indeed, differential economic growth rates manifested in emerging and declining regions reflect less the failure of the marketplace to produce an optimal spatial ordering of economic activity than simply an absence of specific spatial and structural allegiances.

Much of the ongoing debate surrounding the issues of regional growth and decline and industrial change is premised on the notion that the rapid development of some areas or industries while others stagnate or decline is somehow "unfair." But the issues of regional and industrial change are not overwhelmingly issues of equity, although conventional wisdom and its preoccupation with maximizing economic efficiency subject to certain equity concerns seems to have constrained the debate to arguments over which policy interventions produce a more socially desirable outcome. As the discussion in Chapters 1 and 2 emphasizes, however, the growth of the Sunbelt can be viewed mainly in terms of long-run income convergence within a major economic and political system, that system being the United States as a whole. For the most part, the migration of people and jobs is occurring in response to real economic forces affecting the costs of production and service delivery. The result has been to increase the overall efficiency and productivity of the national economy.

This is not to suggest that chronically depressed areas are undeserving of special attention. But if the federal government attempts to prevent the decline of particular areas or industries through the implementation of explicit regional growth or reindustrialization policies, the free movement of factors of production may be interfered with and resources will be employed in less efficient uses.

In any event, concerns over regional and industrial change may become increasingly irrelevant, the current debate over industrial policy notwithstanding. When twenty-first-century historians begin to assess the last third of this century, they will no doubt be struck by the frequency with which contemporary pundits, academics, and journalists declared every U.S. election or political development a watershed in the nation's history. In reality, they will note, only one true "sea change" occurred between 1960 and 2000, with the tide shifting in the early 1980s.

The present time represents a break with the past, or at least a change in the direction of our political economy, because the political consensus, broadly defined, is moving dramatically from a concern with equity to a concern with efficiency. The seeds for this redirection were sown in the 1960s and 1970s. During the 1960s and into the early 1970s, the major goal of public policy was redistributive equity. While it remains unclear whether any meaningful redistribution of income, wealth, or property rights occurred during that period and subsequently, every program from the Equal Employment Opportunity Commission to Model Cities can nonetheless be viewed as a quest for greater social equity.

If the 1960s can be considered the decade of redistribution, the 1970s will be remembered as the decade of crisis management. The Vietnam War bequeathed an overheated, inflationary economy that was increasingly susceptible to exogenous shocks. For example, a run on the dollar early in the decade necessitated the abandonment of fixed exchange rates and a drastic devaluation of the dollar. In essence, the Europeans and Japanese made it clear that they would no longer tolerate the exportation of the United States' inflationary monetary and fiscal policies through the mechanism of an overvalued dollar. Consequently, domestic inflation accelerated to such a point that wage and price controls were imposed for the first time since World War II. Additional inflationary pressures resulted from the two major OPEC price hikes during the 1970s, although the 1979 increase was not so disruptive as the one in 1974.

A corollary to redistributive policies in the 1960s and crisis management in the 1970s was a virtual explosion in the size and scope of government intervention in the marketplace. Government's share of the gross national product (GNP) jumped from 26 percent in 1960 to 33 percent in 1980, and other forms of governmental intrusions—such as regulations, mandates, directives, and court decisions—proliferated over this period. The number of major regulatory agencies rose by nearly 50 percent during the 1970s, and total spending by these agencies increased fourfold. The *Federal Register* expanded from twenty thousand pages in 1970 to eighty thousand in 1980, and the *Code of Federal Regulations* grew by 72 percent to ninety thousand pages in 1980.

Social, economic, technologic, and demographic trends helped to frame a policy environment receptive to additional governmental intrusions during the 1960s and 1970s. Sputnik prompted a much larger federal role in education as a means of closing the perceived knowledge gap. Additional federal aid to education accompanied the arrival of the "baby boom" generation in public schools. The recognition of urban poverty as a major national problem led to higher welfare outlays and new programs to revitalize cities. Environmental protection moved to the top of the political agenda around 1970, not so much because of environmental deterioration as because of the popularization of scientific evidence illustrating the adverse effects of pollution and a growing perception that government should do something about it. Unfortunately, the long-term impacts of many of the new programs and regulations were given only cursory consideration at the time of enactment, and the alleged benefits to be derived from these interventions were not carefully weighed against the costs. In particular, the linkages between regulation, inflation, and productivity were largely ignored.

Not surprisingly, the nation's economic performance during the 1970s deteriorated. In the 1960s, real GNP grew by 46 percent; but during the 1970s it grew by only 33 percent. Industrial output increased 68 percent during the 1960s but only 40 percent during the 1970s. Consumer prices rose an incredible 95 percent in the 1970s compared with a 24 percent rise in the 1960s.

The 1970s also witnessed a drastic erosion of the international competitive position of the United States, despite the depreciation of the dollar. As late as 1969, we enjoyed world dominance in new technologies and new products. During the 1970s, however, concerted efforts by foreign producers, combined with falling productivity, high prices, and quality control problems in U.S. firms, began to undermine seriously the competitive performance of U.S. industry. For example, between 1959 and 1978 the U.S. share of world exports of manufactured goods declined from 25.3 percent to 17 percent. Steel, automobiles, aluminum, textiles, shoes and leather goods, consumer electronics, and many other products began to face serious competition in both domestic and overseas markets. The domestic production of radios, black and white televisions, sewing machines, and watches came to a halt.

By the late 1970s, economists and politicians from various points on the ideological spectrum were arguing that the nation's dismal productivity performance was directly linked to the growth of governmental intervention in the marketplace over the previous two decades. Compliance with regulations and mandates from agencies such as the Environmental Protection Agency (EPA) and the Occupational Safety and Health Administration (OSHA) was resulting in higher production costs and higher consumer prices. Much of the investment required by regulation, such as pollution control devices, was found to be unproductive in that it neither enhanced industry capacity nor added to the productivity of the work force. In addition, funds allocated to meet government mandates were depleting the supply of capital available for capacity-enchancing investments and private research and development activities. The financing of $360 billion of federal budget deficits for the support of social programs during the 1970s was blamed for the ratcheting of interest rates to historic highs and the "crowding out" of many private investors from the capital markets. The revival of economic growth, the experts argued, would require a set of policy initiatives designed to stimulate allocative efficiency and entrepreneurship. First and foremost, it was necessary to reduce governmental interference with private decision making.

Ronald Reagan embraced these themes fervently during the 1980 presidential campaign. Big government and high taxes, he asserted, formed the basis of the nation's economic malaise. Apparently, he struck a responsive chord with most U.S. voters. His landslide victory, coupled with the Republican capture of the Senate and the defeat of many liberal Democrats in both houses, gave a strong signal that a political "sea change" was truly in progress.

On February 18, 1981, after less than a month in office, President Reagan proposed a comprehensive program to revitalize the economy. The centerpiece was a three-year, 25 percent personal income tax cut coupled with liberalized depreciation allowances and tax credits for businesses. Congress passed the Economic Recovery Tax Act, encompassing virtually all of the president's tax proposals, with bipartisan support.

The administration has also achieved considerable success in reducing the growth of federal spending and deregulating several important sectors of the economy, most notably transportation and banking.

Another theme of the Reagan administration has been governmental decentralization, in particular the return of fiscal and functional responsibilities to state and local governments. Reagan would like to see the federal government eventually abandon the social services area except for Social Security and Medicare/Medicaid. Addressing the National Conference of State Legislators on July 30, 1981, President Reagan stated that "the ultimate objective of the New Federalism is to use block grants as a bridge leading to the day when you will have not only the responsibility for programs that properly belong at the state level, but you'll have the tax sources now usurped by Washington returned to you—ending that round trip of people's money to Washington and back minus a carrying charge."

While much of the proposed New Federalism has not been enacted to date, a form of de facto new federalism has come about through severe cuts in federal grants in aid to state and local governments.

THE REGIONAL CONTEXT

From the regional perspective, the public policy problems of growth and decline are more compelling than they are at the larger national level. It is within each of the individual regions that the effects (desirable or undesirable) of change will be more homogeneously felt. In contrast to the political and economic pressures arising in the national arena, such pressures at the regional level are rarely a zero-sum game: some areas may gain, while others (at least relatively) may lose. Whether a given region is facing the discouragement of an extended financial decline or the ebullience of a long-awaited economic renaissance, its residents, its businesses, and its governments are infrequently prepared to disregard their own individual circumstances and adopt an altruistic (or politically compromising) "larger view" of the situation in favor of some perceived "overall" good.

Continued demographic migration seems likely to bring about a further shift of younger, better educated, more highly skilled workers (and households) from the industrial Northeast-Midwest to the South and West. Despite certain implications from the popular press, however, this shift, while substantial, will not reach cataclysmic proportions. Nevertheless, its effects on both migrant-losing and migrant-gaining areas are significant. The exodus from the Midwest deprives that region of important economic resources and needed leadership capabilities.

In the wake of these departures, greater proportions of the remaining populations will be composed of less advantaged (and therefore less geographically mobile) households, thus adding to the region's relative needs as its human capital resources become somewhat depleted. The generally deteriorating economic base, moreover, exacerbates the fiscal and economic difficulties of the region by contributing less to both private sector employment opportunities and public sector revenues, which are ever the more pressed by economic recession.

Such interregional economic and demographic adjustments to changing circumstances tend to be self-limiting at both ends of the migration stream. While demand pressures may be eased in one region, they are increased in others. This is surely being exhibited now in the booming Sunbelt, where the historically low cost of living is approaching the U.S. average as the traditionally atypical subregions of the Sunbelt come more and more to resemble the nation as a whole. These differences may be expected to narrow still further under pressure from the income-elastic demand for more energy, land, capital, manpower, and tax-supported public services throughout the region.

Sunbelt-Frostbelt Truce

By 1980, the Sunbelt-Frostbelt wars of the 1970s had quieted down, and in retrospect it is easy to see why. The controversy really began in the aftermath of the OPEC-induced recession of 1973–75. The industrial heartland of the Northeast and Midwest was especially hard hit, and unemployment rates climbed to the highest levels in thirty-five years. With GNP dropping precipitously, the regions began to battle over a shrinking economic pie. Between 1977 and 1980, however, the economy recovered and all regions of the nation posted economic gains. Regional concerns became less dominant in the public policy forum.

Curiously, the 1981–82 recession did not rekindle the Sunbelt-Frostbelt controversy, probably because the economic dislocations were more geographically dispersed. While unemployment rates in the states composing the traditional manufacturing belt surged, the formerly immune Sunbelt states also suffered, particularly those tied to the health of the energy sector. This convergence of unemployment rates gives strong testimony to the increasing interregional dependency of the national economy.

Despite the recent ebb of the Sunbelt-Frostbelt controversy, regional tensions are likely to resurface and become increasingly important in view of the public policy shift of emphasis to economic efficiency rather than redistributive equity. Inevitably, a structural adjustment guided by market forces will work to the benefit of some places and the detriment of others. Too, shifting the funding for social services back to the states from Washington will also upset regional tranquility. The distribution of needy people is not proportional to the distribution of population, and fiscal capacities and benefit levels vary tremendously among states and regions. Just as states now compete for new business by cutting taxes, under the New Federalism they may also be tempted to pursue beggar-thy-neighbor policies on the spending side, such as cutting welfare benefits in the expectation that low-income people will move to states where benefits are higher.

Energy Taxation: The Newest War Between the States

Without doubt, the most explosive regional issue of the 1980s will be the conflicting concerns of energy-producing and energy-consuming states. The popular press speaks of "energy haves" and "energy have-nots." Politicians from consuming states bemoan the "unfair tax windfalls" to producing states, while those in producing states claim their economic future is being sacrificed to heat homes in Minneapolis or provide electricity to Detroit. Legislation has been introduced in Congress that would impose a federal limitation on state-imposed energy taxes, and both *Business Week* and the Northeast-Midwest Congressional Coalition have called for a national severance tax on energy resources in lieu of individual state taxes.

Some of the consuming states are complaining of severe economic consequences from escalating energy costs and the attendant revenue gains to energy producers. They worry that the producing states will use their energy revenues to fuel even more economic growth at the expense of the energy have-nots by holding down taxes on businesses and individuals. The recently proposed New Federalism has also heightened regional tensions over the severance tax issue because consuming states believe that taking over social programs will be difficult for them and relatively easy for producing states whose rising severance tax receipts will more than compensate for the federal revenue losses. Not to be outdone, many consuming states have been looking for new ways to tax the income of energy companies downstream. For example, New York and Connecticut have enacted gross receipts taxes on oil companies operating in their states, with a prohibition against passing the taxes on to consumers. (Lower courts have struck down this provision in both states, and the cases are on appeal.)

The popular notion that severance taxes are shifted forward to consumers, which is the principal justification for federally imposed limits, has gone virtually unchallenged in the policy debate. At the same time, severance tax "hawks" in some of the producing states claim the tax can be raised substantially without significantly reducing production levels. Both views are wrong. Furthermore, predictions of a several-hundred-billion-dollar transfer of wealth from the energy have-nots to the energy haves over the next decade have been based on extremely simplistic assumptions. In general, the assumptions are that both real prices of energy resources and demand for energy will rise ad infinitum. The experience of the last several years suggests this is not the case; indeed, price increases for energy may well trail the overall inflation rate during the coming decade.

It is also worth noting that severance tax receipts do not always rise. For example, severance tax revenues from oil production in Texas actually fell between fiscal years 1976 and 1977 because the drop in production offset the increase in the average price per barrel. In 1983, lower prices coupled with lower production reduced the severance tax yield once again. If world oil prices remain relatively stable in real terms during the years ahead, declining production in Texas and other oil states will inevitably result in lower severance tax collections.

A federal limitation or preemption of state taxing authority would pose serious constitutional questions, and any legislative initiatives of this nature would surely be challenged in the Supreme Court. Such clearly discriminatory public policy would also fan the fires of economic sectionalism, driving a deeper wedge between the energy-producing and energy-consuming regions of the nation.

Resolving regional energy disputes will not be easy, because energy plays such a critical and complex role in the economies of all regions. Severance taxes themselves are not the real issue. The real issue is higher energy prices, a factor no state, region, or nation can influence to a great degree. Clearly, rising energy costs have imposed severe hardships in some areas of the country; but these hardships have not been confined to any single state or region. Thus, the notion of "winners" and "losers" in the energy game is highly misleading.

CONCLUSION

Regionalism has been a recurring theme in the economic history of the United States. Indeed, the Civil War itself is best understood in strict economic terms. Slaves represented the bulk of the South's productive capital, and a large portion of the region's income was attributable to the productivity of this peculiar institution. Southern slaveowners felt threatened by the election of a Republican president and saw seccesion as a means of protecting their economic interests.

The populist movement of the late nineteenth century also had regional overtones. Populism's greatest appeal was in the rural South and Great Plains, areas not participating in the industrial revolution. Populist politicans promised to protect the "little people" from exploitation by "northern monoplies."

For eighty years after the Civil War, the North and South differed over tariff policy, with the South favoring free trade because much of its agricultural production was exported. The North, on the other hand, wanted to protect its growing industries and saw high tariffs as a means of restricting manufactured imports until its industries could achieve economies of scale. Of course, high tariffs remained long after economies of scale had been realized. The resurgence of protectionist sentiment in the 1980s has also stemmed principally from northern industries and labor unions faced with structural decline.

History has shown that extended real economic growth will do more to defuse regional confrontation than any specific public policy interventions. Thus, we have argued in this book against regional or industrial targeting of governmental aid. Assisting truly *distressed* regions, of course, is a somewhat different issue. But even here there are many unresolved questions. Should aid be directed at places or persons? Creating jobs will not lower unemployment rates if human resources are not simultaneously upgraded. Also, regional economic development does not necessarily lead to the alleviation of poverty. This is most evident in the southern and southwestern states where rapid economic development during the 1970s did not significantly reduce extensive rural poverty. Furthermore, a chronically distressed region may suddenly find its fortunes reversed by changing external circumstances. For example, the OPEC oil embargo did more to revive Appalachia than ten years and $10 billion of federal aid.

The first edition of this book, published in 1978, was subtitled "The Rise of the Sunbelt and the Decline of the Northeast." In 1984, a more appropriate subtitle might be "Clouds over the Sunbelt while the North Rises Again." Today, New England is booming, while many southern and mountain states are in the economic doldrums. And in recent years, the convergence of regional per capita incomes has slowed considerably In fact, as late as 1983, only one Sunbelt state—California—recorded disposable per capita income more than 1 percent above the national average.

Since 1980, eight Sunbelt states have experienced net out-migration while five northern states have shown net in-migration. Ten of the sixteen Sunbelt states lost jobs during the 1980–83 period, while seven of the Frostbelt states posted employment gains. The Sunbelt is also experiencing structural adjustment in declining industries, most notably oil refining, petrochemicals, shipbuilding, and steel.

As the United States moves further into what is sometimes called a postindustrial society, the Frostbelt will be able to capitalize on its legacy of investment in human capital. Indeed, the resurgence of New England can be best explained by the high level of aptitude and functional literacy among its workforce, a reflection of first-class public schools as well as top-notch universities. Most of the Sunbelt states, by contrast, are just now beginning to invest seriously in their educational systems, an investment that will not pay off for at least a decade.

In short, simplistic analyses and statements about the economic health and outlook for the United States' geographic subregions should be eschewed by journalists, politicians and academics. Furthermore, when discussing regional growth and decline, we must keep in mind that the terms are relative, not absolute. We must also avoid the mindset that believes economic growth is a zero-sum game—that one region's gain is another's loss.

A rising tide will, eventually, float all ships. If the national economy can continue along its recent path of real growth with low inflation, all regions of the nation will benefit.

About the Authors

BERNARD L. WEINSTEIN has been assistant director for research and policy at the John Gray Institute of Lamar University in Beaumont, Texas, since January 1983. From 1975 to 1983 he was a professor of economics at the University of Texas at Dallas. He studied public administration at Dartmouth College and received his A.B. in 1963. After a year of graduate study at the London School of Economics, he began graduate work in economics at Columbia University, receiving an M.A. in 1966 and a Ph.D. in 1973.

Dr. Weinstein has authored or coauthored several dozen articles and monographs in the fields of economic development, public policy, and taxation. His work has appeared in such professional journals as *Land Economics*, *Challenge*, *National Civic Review*, *Society*, *Annals of Regional Science*, and *Journal of Legislation*. He has been a contributing editor of *Texas Business*, *Dallas–Fort Worth Business*, and *Texas Banker*.

Dr. Weinstein has been a consultant to many public and private organizations, and his clients have included Texas Instruments, the U.S. Conference of Mayors, the City of Dallas, the City of San Antonio, the Joint Economic Committee of the U.S. Congress, Conoco, and the National Institute of Education. He is president of the Western Tax Association and serves on the intergovernmental fiscal relations committee of the National Tax Association.

Dr. Weinstein served as scholar-in-residence with the Southern Growth Policies Board in Washington, D.C., during 1978–79 and as the board's associate director for federal affairs from 1979 to 1980. During 1980–81 he was director of the Task Force on the Southern Economy of the 1980 Commission on the Future of the South.

HAROLD T. GROSS has been an economist and policy analyst at the John Gray Institute of Lamar University in Beaumont, Texas, since September 1983. From 1982 to 1983 he was a teaching assistant in the School of Social Sciences at the University of Texas at Dallas.

He studied business and public administration at the University of Texas at Dallas and received his B.S. in 1981. He remained at the university for graduate work in political economy, receiving an M.A. in 1982 and a Ph.D. in 1984.

Dr. Gross' current research and policy interests include economic development, industrial organization, and industrial policy. He has authored or coauthored a number of policy studies in the fields of industrial development and regional economic change for clients in both the public and private sectors. His work has appeared in *Challenge*, one of the nation's leading magazines of economic affairs, as well as in the popular media, including *Texas Business* and the *Houston Chronicle*.

JOHN REES is an associate professor of geography in the Maxwell School of Citizenship and Public Affairs at Syracuse University in Syracuse, New York. From 1975 to 1983 he was on the political economy faculty of the University of Texas at Dallas. He received his B.A. from the University of Wales, his M.A. from the University of Cincinnati, and his Ph.D. from the London School of Economics.

Dr. Rees has written over forty journal articles, book chapters and reports on industrial location and the impact of technological change on regional development. He has been consultant to the Joint Economic Committee of the U.S. Congress, the Department of Housing and Urban Development, the General Accounting Office, the Office of Technology Assessment, the John Gray Institute, and the International Institute for Applied Systems Analysis.